TWICE THE *vows*
TWICE THE *grace*

From Heartbreak
to Healing:
A Marriage
Rebuilt by Grace

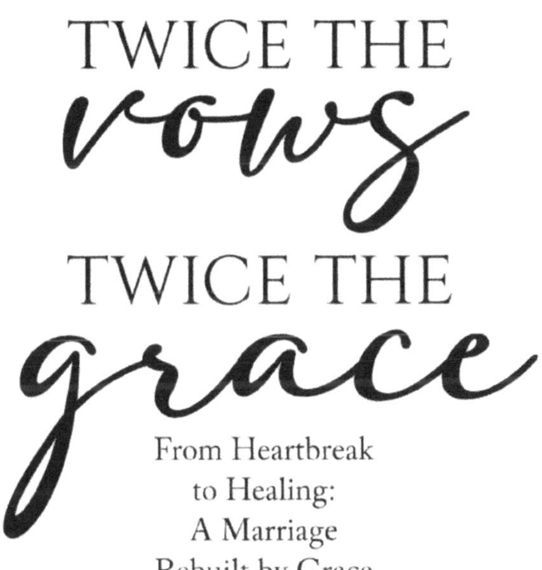

GREGORY L. NAPIER &
CAROLYN L NAPIER

MARRIED
WITH A PURPOSE

An imprint of Married With a Purpose

COPYRIGHTS

Published by: Married With A Purpose

Library of Congress Control Number: 2025921237

ISBN: 979-8-9932166-1-4.
ISBN: 979-8-9932166-0-7

Book Cover by 100 Covers

Book Interior: Luke Adams

Developmental Editor: Colette R. Harrell

First edition 2026

Website: https://www.marriedwithapurpose.com

ACKNOWLEDGMENTS

To God be the glory . . . for His unfailing love, mercy, and grace that carried us through every storm, restored what was broken, and renewed what was lost.

This book stands as a living testimony that what God joins together, no man can truly separate.

We dedicate this work first and foremost to **our Heavenly Father**, whose grace has been more than sufficient, and whose faithfulness has never failed.

To **Jesus Christ,** the center of our marriage, the anchor of our souls, and the reason this story exists. And to the **Holy Spirit,** our guide, our comforter, and our constant reminder that true love is built on forgiveness, humility, and divine purpose.

We also dedicate this book to **every couple** who has walked through pain, betrayal, or loss—may you find hope in our story and the courage to believe that God can rebuild what seems beyond repair.

A legacy of Love to our **children, grandchildren, and great-grandchildren**, you are the living proof of God's grace and the legacy of love that continues through generations.

May you always remember that with God at the center, no obstacle is too great, no wound too deep, and no dream too far gone.

Our prayer is that this story inspires you to love deeply, forgive freely, and trust God's plan even when the path is hard to see.

With all our love,

Pastor Gregory L. Napier & Evangelist Carolyn Napier

"From heartbreak to healing—a marriage rebuilt by grace.

FOREWORD

We all know the term "read 'em and weep." But as an author, a retired director of social services, and a citizen of the Kingdom, this book brought me to tears. I've known Gregory and Carolyn Napier for over twenty years. I've watched them stumble, and I've been a cheerleader as I watched them recover from the eventual fall. They did it all with grace. Divorced and remarried, they share not only what went wrong, but also how to get it right.

When I first met them, Greg wasn't yet a pastor; he was serving as an armor bearer. I have always believed that if you want to know how someone will lead, you should first watch how they follow. Greg was unstoppable. In fact, if anyone were to ask me about his personality, the very first word I would use is *faithful*. That is why seeing him step fully into his calling—and watching him extend that calling through the marriage coaching ministry he shares with Carolyn—has always made perfect sense to me.

My second top attribute to describe Greg would be transparency. Many people who know Greg are nodding. He will tell it like it is, not only on others but on himself. He's actively learning how to spoon his honesty with sugar, but this is where Carolyn comes in.

Carolyn is the only woman I know who is graced to be Greg's helpmate and partner in life. She is one of the calmest, most tranquil individuals I have ever met. She is patient and tactful. She is the balance for Greg that God designed to help him complete his assignments with a gentle hand, not a hammer.

And while she is his earthly compass, she allows him to hear and do the things that God has purposed him to deliver. She never dilutes him or the power that God is using in them to help transform marriages into strong units that will build better communities.

In her own right, Carolyn is accomplished in so many areas. Her gift of administration has helped so many in and outside of the Kingdom. A retired HR manager for a government agency, she is trusted to bring her gifts to various tables.

This book is not only informative but also a lifeline for marriages in the critical care unit (ICU). What do I mean by ICU? After reading this book, I would pen ICU as the *Intentional Care Unit* for your marriage. This book provides a treatment plan that will help you, as a couple, achieve ultimate health. When a marriage is in crisis, it often needs the same level of attention as a patient in intensive care. In the hospital, ICU stands for *Intensive Care Unit,* a place where broken bodies receive round-the-clock care, constant monitoring, and life-saving interventions.

In the same way, this book provides troubled marriages with intentional care, not casual attention or sound bites that only pacify but never cure. Gregory and Carolyn Napier are looking to transform your atmosphere. *You can't heal in the same environment that made you sick.*

This book reminds you that healing requires focus, priority, and urgent action. It means slowing down enough to notice the warning signs, committing to repair rather than retreat, and giving your marriage the best of your energy instead of the leftovers.

The other part of ICU is my personal note to Gregory and Carolyn: *I See You*. What you are bringing to the Kingdom, the way you are showing couples how to rediscover intimacy, communication, and understanding even in their finances, is transformative.

In closing, maybe your marriage is in hospice, and you're awaiting its final call, or you've accepted the diagnosis that your marriage has a long-term illness. And you've settled in your spirit that you have to live with its symptoms, including loneliness. Or you may have already pulled the plug and called the time of death. *Twice the Vows, Twice the Grace* is the prescription for you. Its delivery is simple and speaks to the heart of the matter, with real-life anecdotes, and God at its center. You will receive the resuscitation your marriage needs, one breath at a time.

PRELUDE TO GRACE

In 1978, the R&B Duo Peaches & Herb released a song titled "Reunited." And while everyone snapped their fingers and swayed from side to side, others were wishing, yearning, and wanting to be reunited with someone they had failed to treasure. I understand their pain. My name is Pastor Gregory Napier. I wasn't always a pastor. I wasn't always an upstanding citizen, a good guy. I was a broken man who went around breaking things, including relationships. I was such an expert at it that I broke my marriage. But if I want to help others, the only way to do that is to bring you the unadulterated truth, not just the facts, but the underlying issues of a broken relationship.

Many hidden problems lead up to at least one person in the relationship saying, "Enough!" It was never about the snoring—although the snoring was maddening. It wasn't the dirty clothes consistently strewn around the room, although how difficult is it to pick up after yourself? Instead, it's the turmoil boiling beneath the surface. It's the lies, manipulation, the overspending, the stinginess, the lack of trust, the lack of respect, the lack of communication . . . it's about the lack thereof. I've heard it said, "Never make a decision based on lack. It will always reek of desperation." I've learned the truth in that statement.

Our choices build our futures, and when we make our next decision out of desperation, we invariably choose the wrong one. We place a period and end things when a comma should have been used. Your relationship should be more than poor grammar. Carolyn and I want to give you that opportunity to pause. To take a Selah break in the hurt, confusion, and pain of a relationship in turmoil. We want to share our journey with each of you. The broken valleys and how we made it to the healed mountaintop that we now sit on, and marvel at a God who brought us through, and then assigned us to share the good news that many of you are sitting in valuable property—your marriage—you just have appraised it wrong.

John 8:32 states, "and you will know the truth, and the truth will set you free."

Please listen to what I am saying and understand that transparency is never easy, but it gets easier the more you tell the truth. I think of truth as a muscle, one that, when used diligently, with consistency and also with love and respect, builds strength. Isn't that what a muscle represents? Not sinewy lines of masculinity, but a sign that you have valued your body and that it can hold up under pressure. That you have built it strong. We need strong marriages that build strong families and communities. This book, *Twice the Vows, Twice the Grace*, is your guide to evaluating, rebuilding, and then valuing your marriage. It is anecdotal, where you will find and identify with Carolyn and me somewhere in the issues and the steps to marital redemption.

Come on in and let's get started.

Twice The Vows Twice The Grace

Chapter 1

The Pain of Betrayal and the Miracle of Redemption

Betrayal is a deep wound that festers. It's not just about breaking trust; it's about breaking a heart. Looking back on my life, one of the hardest things I've had to face is deceiving my wife, Carolyn, the woman who loved me more than anyone else in this world. She stood by me through my struggles, addiction, and darkest days. Yet, I destroyed the faith she had in me. Infidelity isn't just about cheating on your spouse; it's about damaging the covenant that you committed to, together. Marriage isn't just a contract; after all, contracts are easily broken. Marriage is a covenant; vows you stood before God and took to forsake all others. This included forsaking the drugs that wove themselves into the fabric of my life.

Let me start by admitting that I turned to drugs to cope with unresolved childhood issues. As a result, I learned to hide my drug use. I was a pro at it; I'd been hiding one way or another my whole life. And Carolyn didn't know, and I wasn't sharing. What I didn't realize was that I was in deeper than I thought. I believed I could handle it. But drugs were taking over my life. Addiction is like a thief in the night; it steals everything from you before you even realize it's missing. It snatched my self-control, honesty, and my ability to be a good husband. It made me selfish, and in that selfishness, I made the worst mistake of my life.

Carolyn had already gone through the roller coaster of a broken relationship. She had two boys from her previous marriage, and she worked hard to raise them right. When we got married, I knew I was not just marrying her. I was becoming part of a family. My goal was to restore what had been taken and make our family whole.

But addiction doesn't care about your goals, love, or your plans for your family. It blinds you to what really matters.

In the middle of my addiction, I made a choice that changed everything. I was unfaithful to Carolyn, and because of my sin, a child was conceived—a baby, a life born from my selfish actions. (The sin was mine, not my child's.) When I found out, I felt like the ground had been ripped out from under me. There was a constant weight in the pit of my stomach, and I couldn't get rid of it. The guilt was heavy, but not as heavy as the pain I saw in Carolyn's eyes when she learned the truth.

She didn't scream or curse. I couldn't read her facial expressions, which changed so quickly from bad to worse that I closed my eyes to the damage I had caused. That face still haunts me, revealing the hollow pain that hits when the person you love most wounds you to your core. She had given me her all when she placed her hand in mine in marriage, and I had thrown it all away for a moment of weakness. Her eyes spoke louder than any shouting she could have done, and I was the one who lost the ability to murmur one more word of apology.

According to the General Social Survey, about 20 percent of married men admit to having had sex with someone other than their spouse.[1] That may seem like just a number, but behind that number are real people, families, extended families, and communities in real pain. According to the "Reasons for Divorce" study conducted by Scott, Rhoades, Stanley, Allen, and Markman, infidelity was cited as a

---

[1] General Social Survey (GSS), "Marital Infidelity Data," Institute for Family Studies, accessed 2025

significant contributing factor in divorce by 59.6 percent of individuals and by at least one partner in 88.8 percent of couples.[2] It's important to note that being cited as a contributor doesn't mean infidelity alone caused the divorce. It implies that unfaithfulness played a significant role in the breakdown of the marriage.

I didn't know the odds at the time. But what I *did* know was that my marriage was hanging by a thread.

And then it happened. Carolyn filed for divorce. She had given me chance after chance, but this level of betrayal was too much. What I haven't mentioned is that Carolyn gave me multiple opportunities to get things right. Instead, I kept bringing drama into our relationship. It was becoming toxic. This book can't go back and list all the damage I caused. But my commitment to transparency pushes me to admit some of my misdeeds: I got arrested on a trip in Georgia. I cashed a government check that had been mailed to our house, made out to Carolyn. When she asked if I had seen the check, I lied and said I hadn't. I would pick fights so that I could go out and do drugs. Criminality, theft, manipulation, lies, and gaslighting. It's not a pretty list, and it's not comprehensive.

She had to protect herself, her heart, and her boys. The divorce wasn't just a legal decision; it was what we both felt was a final break, a reality check that my actions had consequences.

The day our divorce was final, I felt like I had lost everything. It wasn't just about losing my wife; I had lost my best friend, my family, my home. Addiction had cost me everything that truly mattered. Some people hit rock bottom once. I felt like over my lifetime, I had hit it repeatedly, but this hit differently. This was the lowest point of my existence.

---

[2] Scott et al., "Infidelity in Committed Relationships, Psychological Bulletin (2013)

I had to face a hard truth: Carolyn was gone, and I was alone.

The scene of the day the truth was revealed is etched in my memory and repeats like an old LP on replay.

The kitchen was quiet except for the low hum of the refrigerator. Carolyn sat at the table, her hands folded neatly in front of her, the glow of the overhead light casting shadows across her face. Her expression was unreadable, but her stillness was heavy, like the air before a storm.

I stood by the counter, leaning back as though distance could minimize the moment's seriousness. But my sweating palms were a reminder that I had messed up—badly. My throat felt dry, and every word I tried to muster felt like I might shatter the fragile silence.

"I swear, Carolyn," I started, my voice shaky but desperate, "It—it didn't mean anything. It was a mistake. A terrible mistake."

Her eyes lifted to meet mine, slow and deliberate. Deep brown, flecked with molten gold, they had once held love. Now, they were unreadable pools of sorrow, glowing with a pain that burned hotter than anger. It seemed as though every time she blinked, her expression changed. I was losing track of her unfamiliar cycle of anger, rage, hurt, disbelief, repeating over and over. Then, before speaking, it stilled.

"You didn't just make a mistake, Gregory," she said, her voice calm but carrying the weight of a thousand unspoken emotions. "You made a choice."

"I know, I know!" I stammered, stepping toward her as if now moving closer might somehow close the chasm between us. "I was weak. I wasn't thinking straight. I was high; that's what messed me up. You know this isn't-wasn't my fault."

Her gaze never wavered. "No, this was all on you. Addiction doesn't make choices for you. It doesn't climb into someone else's bed. You did that."

I winced. Her words were soft, but they struck with the force of a hammer. "It was like I was in a fog, and then I wasn't," I whispered. "I . . . I never set out to do this."

She nodded slowly, as though considering my words. "And yet, here we are."

I ran a hand down my face and over my beard, its prickly feel underscoring my lack of a shave that morning, and I started pacing the small kitchen like a caged animal. "I didn't know about the baby until much later, I swear. God help me for the thoughts that ran through my mind as I tried to wish this away, but I can't, and I'm sorry. But, baby, we can get through this."

Her lips pressed into a thin line. She looked down at her hands, the wedding ring still on her finger. She twisted it absentmindedly, then stopped, her hands still once more.

"You made promises, Greg. We made promises. Vows," she said, her voice faltering only slightly. "Not just to me, but to my boys. To this family, before God. Do you even understand what you've done?"

"I do," I cried, the desperation bubbling to the surface. "I know I've broken everything, but I can fix it. Please, Carolyn. I'll do whatever it takes. Therapy, rehab, anything. Just don't give up on us."

She exhaled slowly, the kind of breath that felt like it carried years of buried expectations. "This isn't about giving up," she said quietly. "It's about survival. Mine. The boys. You brought chaos into this house. All I tried to do was create a place of peace. You have finally made me do the one thing I said I'd never do—" Her voice cracked, but she steadied herself. Shaking her head, she said, "Now, there's a child. A child who will forever remind me of what you did. How am I supposed to live with that?"

No longer prideful, I dropped to my knees in front of her, reaching for her hands. She didn't pull away, but her fingers remained limp in mine. "Carolyn, I love you," I said, my voice breaking. "You are everything to me. I can't lose you. I can't lose us."

She stood slowly, gently pulling her hands away from mine. "I need some time, Greg," she said, her tone as final as a judge's gavel. "Can you leave? I need to think."

I sat there on the cold tile floor, the silence rushing back to fill the space she had left. Betrayal is a wound that cuts deeply, but you survive. This didn't feel that way; it felt like a final blow, a mortal one.

Looking back, I almost wished she had screamed, even cursed. Maybe then I could have contrived some self-righteous anger. But instead, I had to confront a harsh truth: Carolyn was gone, and I was on my own.

Listen to our Podcast #17 on Apple or Spotify: Why Your Marriage Isn't Growing/How We Rebuilt Trust in Our Christian Marriage after Betrayal

Link: https://why-your-marriage-isnt-growing.captivate.fm/

Chapter 2

Carolyn's Pain—Living with Unfaithfulness
The Moment My Heart Shattered

Gone. Not physically, not yet. But emotionally, I had already left the marriage long before we had signed the divorce papers.

When I first found out about Greg's infidelity, I didn't react the way most women might. I didn't cry or perform. I didn't throw things or demand answers. I just . . . shut down.

I hadn't planned it that way; it just happened. It was like my body kept going, but my heart had stopped. I felt like I was walking through my own life like a ghost, there, but not really. My world had been flipped upside down, and yet, no one could see it.

To outsiders, I was the same Carolyn. I still went to work. I still took care of my boys. I still functioned. But inside? Inside, I was breaking.

Unfaithfulness isn't just about the act; it's about what it does to you as a person. We enter relationships to add value to our lives. His cheating subtracted. It took away trust that was already eroding. It eliminated intimacy. It stripped us of honest communication. The lies, manipulation, and carelessness had built up to the point I could not reason. It took away my ability to think.

I had spent years believing in my husband, standing by him through his addiction, praying for his deliverance. I had fought for him, defended him, held onto hope when no one else did. And for what? For him to willfully destroy the very thing I spent years protecting.

I felt like a fool.

I was silently suffering. Greg could not read me. He knew me, but he didn't see how deep the pool of anguish ran. I was drowning. I wasn't a crier, so he had no tears to trace the road map of hurt. Yet the pain lived in my body, etched into the slump of my posture, no longer upright but bent beneath the weight of defeat.

Psychologist Dennis C. Ortman articulated what many affected spouses already knew in their bones. In 2005, he introduced the term Post-Infidelity Stress Disorder (PISD) in the Journal of Psychosocial Nursing and Mental Health Services. He drew the line straight and pinpointed the devastation of betrayal to Post-Traumatic Stress Disorder (PTSD). He wanted the world to understand that discovering a partner's unfaithfulness is not a minor heartbreak; it's a life-altering wound that carves itself into memory, trust, and self-worth. And the numbers bear it out.[3]

A 2006 study by Steffens and Rennie found that nearly 70 percent of participants met the criteria for PTSD after experiencing infidelity. They did not meet the technical definition of "Criterion A" in the DSM, exposure to death, serious injury, or sexual violence, but their minds and bodies told another story.[4] Their hearts pounded, their nights fractured with sleeplessness, flashbacks, and suspicion haunted their days. What Ortman named PISD captures this reality: cheating leaves scars that look and feel like trauma. Infidelity is not a simple lapse in judgment; it is devastation dressed in human skin. It dismantles your feelings of safety. It rewrites the story of love. It

---

[3] Dennis Ortman, Post-Infidelity Stress Disorder (Rowman & Littlefield, 2005)
[4] Steffens, B. A., & Rennie, R. L. (2006). The traumatic nature of disclosure for wives of sexual addicts. Sexual Addiction & Compulsivity

turns the familiar into foreign and the trusted into a threat. For the deceived, life after cheating is not just sadness—it is a fight for survival.

I couldn't sleep. My mind was constantly racing, replaying everything over and over again.

How long had he been lying to me?

How many times had he looked me in the eyes and

chosen deception over truth?

Was there something wrong with me? Had I not been

enough?

How much more didn't I know?

I knew logically that Greg's choices were his own, that his addiction had led him down this path. But logic doesn't erase emotion. And addiction doesn't erase consequences.

I began to withdraw, not out of anger, but out of necessity. I couldn't let Greg break me any further than he already had.

He would speak to me, and I would barely respond. I would go through the motions of our life, but inside, I felt nothing.

It was a numbness that scared me.

In their article "Love and Infidelity: Causes and Consequences," Ami Rokach and Sybil H. Chan report that betrayed spouses are significantly more likely to experience anxiety, depression, and even suicidal thoughts.[5] Their research underscores what so many already

---

[5] Ami Rokach and Sybil Chan, "Love and Infidelity: Causes and Consequences," International Journal of Environmental Research and Public Health 20, no. 3 (2023)

know by experience: infidelity is not a private mistake; it carries a public cost in mental, emotional, and even physical health.

I never wanted to die, but I wanted the pain to stop. I tried to wake up, hoping this was all a bad dream. But it wasn't a dream. It was my reality.

I now felt we were a marriage built on lies. One of the worst parts of betrayal is realizing that your entire relationship was built on a foundation that wasn't as solid as you thought. I had believed in our love. I had believed in Greg.

I had married this man with the full expectation that we would walk through life together, that no matter how hard things got, we would always choose each other. And yet, he hadn't chosen me.

He had chosen addiction.

He had chosen secrecy.

He had chosen another woman.

I didn't know how to exist in a marriage where I felt like a second choice. It had become an unseen battle that I didn't realize I was fighting.

People think that when a woman finds out about infidelity, she's supposed to react a certain way. But what most people don't realize is that the deepest pain is often the quietest.

I remember sitting alone in our bedroom one night, just staring at the wall. Greg was in the next room, probably wondering what I was thinking, but he never asked. He was scared of the answer. So, he was walking on eggshells, and I had no desire to remove them. Why should I? I'm no saint.

I wanted to scream at him, "You did this! You destroyed everything! Do you even care?"

But I didn't. Because at this point, what would it change?

I wasn't interested in apologies. I didn't want excuses. I didn't even want him to explain why he did it. I just wanted to feel whole again.

Infidelity is a painful experience that can profoundly affect a woman's self-esteem. Discovering that a partner has cheated can shatter her sense of trust, worth, and identity. In their article "Love and Infidelity: Causes and Consequences," the authors examine the emotional toll of betrayal, demonstrating how infidelity harms self-perception and personal value. Their work underscores the long journey many women face—from betrayal to eventual empowerment—as they rebuild confidence and reclaim their identity.

I was one of them. For the first time in my life, I doubted everything about myself.

Was I not pretty enough?

Was I not a good enough wife?

Did I do something to push him away?

I knew deep down that I had been a good wife. I had

stood by him through his worst moments. I had loved him even when his addiction made him impossible to love. And still, he had stepped out of our marriage bed.

Ultimately, I chose to leave. Some women stay. Some women forgive. But I couldn't, not yet.

Numerous studies reveal that 60–75 percent of couples remain married after an affair. [6]

---

[6] S. D. Solomon and L. J. Teagno, Intimacy after Infidelity; K. Nickerson, R. Stone, and R. Davies, Affair Attitudes Survey

Yes, most marriages do survive. Some limp along, never quite healing. Others get the help they need to reconnect—sometimes by working with coaches like Gregory and me. But at that point in my life, I couldn't join the majority who chose to stay. I wanted out.

Filing for divorce wasn't an easy decision, but it was the only one I felt I had left. I couldn't live in a house where I felt invisible. I couldn't share a bed with a man who had shared himself with someone else.

Leaving wasn't about punishing Greg; it was about saving myself.

The day I left, I didn't cry. I packed my things, took my boys, and walked out the door. I had planned to move out while Greg wasn't home. He returned as we were loading the final load. Greg was silent. He knew he had lost me. He knew there was nothing he could say to undo what had been done.

That night, I sat alone in my new place and, for the first time, I allowed myself to feel everything.

The anger.

The sadness.

The heartbreak.

I had spent so much time holding it all in, trying to be strong, but now, there was no reason to.

And so, I let it out. Not in tears. Not in screams. But in the quiet realization that my marriage was over.

The hardest part wasn't leaving. It wasn't even the betrayal itself. The hardest part was learning how to be Carolyn again.

For five years, I had been Greg's faithful wife. His supporter. His fighter. The one who held it all together. Now, I had to figure out who I was without him.

Research shows that divorce due to infidelity often leads to an identity crisis, especially for women who are deeply invested in the marriage (Ricardo Nicastro, "How Infidelity Shatters a Couple's Shared Identity," Dec 2024).[7] The betrayal severs the emotional ties to rituals and symbols that once nurtured the couple's shared identity. What was once familiar now feels foreign. The betrayed partner may feel alienated from the very practices that once defined their connection, deepening the grief and estrangement. When this shared identity is shattered, the couple loses the emotional anchor that once held them together. Instability follows, and with it comes a cascade of emotional and psychological challenges. For the betrayed partner, the fallout is profound. That was me.

I had given everything to Greg, and now, I had to figure out what was left of me.

People often say that divorce is giving up, but they don't understand that sometimes, walking away is the *only* way to survive. I didn't know at the time that there were ways back to each other. I didn't see a fork in the road. All I saw was the exit sign.

The weight of my pain felt like a chokehold around my neck. I decided that I wanted this to be over as quickly as possible. I thought if I rushed to the end, I could hurry up to the new beginning. I didn't truly comprehend that I was only beginning a very long journey.

---

[7] Ricardo Nicastro, "How Infidelity Shatters a Couple's Shared Identity," Dec 2024

I searched for an attorney who could expedite the process. She gave me a price, and I didn't blink. She said if he is not contesting, it could be done in three weeks.

When she contacted him, he told her he wouldn't contest it. He also added, "Tell her, she can't keep my last name." I believe this request backfired on him and maybe on me as well.

My lawyer was true to her words. The divorce was final in three weeks.

As he demanded, I went back to my maiden name.

Remember, Greg and I worked for the same government agency. As a Human Resources (HR) supervisor, I was responsible for signing many employee notices posted on employee bulletin boards. Divorce is embarrassing. It is a statement to others that you couldn't make your marriage work.

My private humiliation was about to become public.

One of the things I had wanted was to keep our situation private. But it was out there for everyone to see. I had not even told my staff until I had to do an official name change. Once this change occurred, people began to change toward me, both positively and negatively. For some of my male coworkers, I was back on the market. And for some of my female coworkers, he was, and I was now fuel for gossip. As HR, I had always been privy to their business. For example, whose wages were being garnished. Who was written up and in danger of losing their job. I was the purveyor of their issues, and now they had what they felt was a front-row seat to mine.

It was humbling.

This is what no one tells you about healing. Sometimes, in the process, the scabs will be pulled off. That's what going into work felt like to me on some days. God has a funny way of showing you how even when you think you are doing a thing, you aren't. Here, I wanted to leave him behind, but we worked together. And I could go around him, but I couldn't go around all of our mutual acquaintances and coworkers. It hit me then that this would be a one-step-forward, two-steps-back process. I had only hurried up to wait.

Healing isn't a straight path. Some days, I felt fine. On other days, the pain was unbearable. I had to learn how to trust myself again. I had to learn that Greg's choices did not define my worth. It wasn't a quick fix; it was grueling work that only I could do.

Time is spiritual currency. You can't get it back, but you can redeem it. It's God's supernatural way of honoring your faithfulness because faith without works is dead. So, we must do the work. Everything has a season, and we truly reap what we sow. This was my season of sowing my faith and patience, and of what I felt was long-suffering, which led to my healing and eventually to our reconciliation.

Oh, what a mighty harvest!

***

Healing from betrayal is painful, but possible. It requires time, intentionality, and a commitment to rebuilding trust—not just in others, but in yourself. Here are two actionable steps women can take to move beyond betrayal, with real-life examples of how to apply each.

1. Rebuild Your Self-Worth and Identity

Why It Matters:

Infidelity can make you question your worth: *Was I not enough? Was it something I did? Am I unlovable?* The truth is that someone else's betrayal is not a reflection of your values. Healing means rediscovering your own identity outside of your relationship.

Real-Life Example:

After my husband cheated, I realized I had lost myself in the marriage. I had given up hobbies, stopped seeing friends, and put all my energy into being the "perfect wife." To heal, I started doing things for myself—traveling with friends and volunteering. Each step helped me remember that I was more than just someone's wife—I was a strong, independent woman.

How to Apply It:

- Reconnect with old passions: What did you love before the relationship? Painting, dancing, reading? Start again.

- Try something new: Take a cooking class, travel to a new place, or start a fitness journey.

- Affirm your worth daily: Stand in the mirror and say, "I am worthy. I am enough. I deserve love and respect."

2. Choose Forgiveness—But on Your Own Terms

Why It Matters:

Forgiveness isn't about letting the betrayer off the hook—it's about freeing yourself from the chains of anger and resentment. But forgiveness doesn't mean reconciliation. You can forgive someone and still choose not to let them back into your life.

Real-Life Example:

Greg deeply hurt me. At first, I held onto the pain, replaying the act in my mind daily. But I realized that my anger wasn't punishing him; it was poisoning my own heart. I wrote a letter of forgiveness (but never sent it). I forgave myself, not for him, but for me.

How to Apply It:

- Understand that forgiveness is for you: It's about releasing bitterness so you can move forward.

- Forgive at your own pace: It doesn't have to happen overnight. Give yourself grace.

- Write a forgiveness letter: Regardless of whether you send it, writing down your emotions and expressing your forgiveness can be healing.

One of the joys I found in my new independence was that I started traveling for my job, and it gave me space to find myself again. By traveling to new places, I expanded my vision and found myself not so alone but part of something much bigger. I expanded my network and strengthened other relationships I had neglected. Learning to be me again allowed me to like myself. To appreciate my contributions to my family, work, and friends.

Much later, when Greg and I reconciled, I remained true to who I had created, allowing us to be a strong couple because two whole individuals had entered into it with trust, communication, and love.

Prayer Break

Lord, when I hear from You, I gain clarity.
I can speak to the mountain, and it will move.
What was meant for evil, You turn toward purpose.

I would not have chosen pain,
yet You show me it has meaning—
revealing the sickness so You can guide us to healing.
Even in disappointment, You reveal possibility.

Thank You, Lord.
Amen.

Chapter 3

Carolyn—When God Speaks in the Silence

After the divorce, I was determined to keep moving forward. I kept myself busy with work, responsibilities, and pretending I was fine. I had spent years giving my all to a marriage that had ended, and now, I was trying to piece myself back together.

I was on a work assignment, living in a hotel suite for almost a year. The days were easy enough to get through, and the job kept me distracted. But the nights . . . The nights were unbearable.

I was in the loneliest place. Yes, I had made new friends, rebuilt old ones. But my bed was empty, and my heart was still sore. The scabs were still apparent if you looked hard enough. And if you only asked, I could easily show them to you.

It was a summer evening, and the moonlight was shining in my bedroom. I was lying in bed, staring at the ceiling, listening to the hum of the air conditioner. The room was quiet, but my mind was not. Thoughts of Greg—his deceitfulness—of the life I thought we had built together raced through my head. Heaviness pressed against my chest, making breathing difficult, and I wondered if I would ever feel whole again.

Then, out of silence, I heard a voice.

It wasn't just a thought floating through my consciousness. It was audible, and something far greater than me. Someone's presence had entered the room. It was the unmistakable voice of God.

"Where do you say children come from?" He said, His voice unmistakable in its power and glory.

The question stopped me in my tracks. My heart pounded. I whispered back, as naturally as breathing, "They are a gift from you, God."

Then came the response that shook me to my core. *"Then the child was not a gift from me?"*

I sat up straight in bed, suddenly alert. This child—Greg's son born from his affair—had been a source of so much turmoil for me. He was the proof of everything that had been broken. He was the result of my husband's infidelity, the reminder of a wound that still felt raw.

I wanted to answer, but all that came out was, "But—"

And just like that, not just the voice was gone, but also the presence. The silence in the room was deafening, louder than the voice had been. I felt as if the very presence of God had vanished, leaving me alone with my thoughts.

I cried, "Don't go!"

But there was no response.

I sat there, tears streaming down my face, realizing that I had never once thought about the child outside of my grief at his existence. To me, he had only ever been the consequence of our broken marriage. He hadn't been flesh and blood. He was a catalyst, a symptom of vows gone wrong.

But God . . . God had just asked me something that I wasn't prepared to answer.

I waited in silence every night after that. Each evening, I returned to my hotel room and waited for the voice to return. I longed to hear it again. I needed clarity, understanding, something to hold onto. But all I got was silence.

I wrestled with my emotions, with my anger, with the sheer unfairness of it all. I had spent so much time thinking about what Greg had done to me, how he had shattered my trust and broken our marriage. But now, God had shifted the focus to something I had never considered before.

This baby was an innocent child. And God had chosen me to be part of his story. But I had responded, no.

What had I done?

God's question had changed everything!

Weeks passed before the voice returned. In the quiet of my solitude, I prayed. I worshipped. I read the word of God. Slowly, my acceptance that more change was coming had rendered me malleable.

I was ready.

I had spent those weeks replaying the moment God had entered my room, and I had let Him down. I had thought about the question, about what I truly believed.

When the voice spoke again, I knew I wanted to respond without hesitation, without defensiveness, without *"buts."*

Then in the still of the night, He returned.

"Where do babies come from?"

I answered, "They are a gift from you, God."

Then, He asked, *"Who gives life?"*

I breathed deeply and responded, "You do, God."

And then He asked something I had never even considered:

"Have you ever asked why I chose you?"

Tears welled in my eyes. The truth was, I had never once thought about it. *Why* did *God choose me?*

I had only seen myself as a victim, someone who had been betrayed, abandoned, and hurt. I had spent so much time asking, "Why did Greg do this to me?" that I had never stopped to ask, "What is God doing in this situation?"

The weight of that realization crushed me. I once had bronchitis, and when I finally began to heal, the mucus and congestion began breaking up inside my chest, and after weeks of not being able to cough anything up, it all started to come out. It wasn't pretty, but it was the effect of my healing.

After not screaming or crying during this entire time, I began to weep—buckets of tears. My tears were not just because of the release of the pain, but because I was starting to see things differently. Like phlegm from a bout of bronchitis, it wasn't pretty, but a sign that the ugliness was coming out and that I was healing.

New thoughts entered my consciousness. Maybe this wasn't just about what had been done *to* me. Perhaps this was about what God wanted to do *through* me.

There is a song that states, "*I can see clearly now the rain is gone . . .*" That night changed me. It didn't erase the hurt; it eased it. It shifted my perspective.

I had been so focused on my suffering that I had forgotten about the sovereignty of God. He was the giver of life. He allowed this child to be born. And if God, in His perfect wisdom, let this child come into the world, who was I to reject him?

That didn't mean I suddenly felt no pain. That didn't mean I immediately forgave Greg. Complete healing would still take time.

But something in my heart began to soften.

Instead of only seeing betrayal, I started to see purpose. Instead of only seeing pain, I began to see God's plan.

Maybe, just maybe, God had chosen me for something greater than my hurt.

Slowly, I started to feel like me again.

And then, when I least expected it, something happened that I never thought possible . . .

I saw Greg again—not the man whose actions almost destroyed me, but the man who was fighting to be better.

And for the first time in a long time, I didn't just see him.

I saw hope.

***

What I experienced that night in my hotel room is something I believe every woman who has faced betrayal can relate to. We often get stuck in the pain, in the "why me?" But what if we asked, "God, what do you want me to learn from this?" Would your obedience be better than a later sacrifice?

Here are some takeaways from my encounter with God and my walk of obedience:

God's plan is bigger than our pain.

We may not understand why things happen, but God never wastes our suffering. He redeems broken situations for a greater purpose.

Forgiveness is a process, not an instant decision.

God didn't tell me to forgive Greg that night. He asked me to see the situation from His perspective. Forgiveness came later, but it started with changing the way I saw things. Empathy is a powerful tool toward forgiveness.

God's assignments often come in unexpected ways.

I never would have chosen to be part of the child's life. But God chose me for this assignment, not as a punishment, but as a calling.

We have to be willing to listen, even when it's hard.

God's voice challenged me. It forced me to confront my own bitterness and pain. But it also led me to healing.

I won't pretend that everything changed overnight. Healing took time. But that moment in my hotel room was the turning point.

I had been waiting for Greg to change, waiting for my situation to be different, waiting for time to erase the pain. But what I really needed was to listen to what God was saying to me.

And that's when I began to let go—not of the memory, not of the lesson, but of the weight that had been crushing me.

Maybe, just maybe, betrayal was not the end of my story.

Maybe it was the beginning of something greater.

***

I'm not sure how anyone can reach a place of real healing without God. I'm a Christian, and I believe that it is possible to break down without seeking God in the midst of our trauma. I also know that at some point in the fall, we will cry out, "Jesus."

A soldier on the battlefield once stated, "There are no atheists in foxholes." I would hold that to be true. Every drowning man wants a savior. Here are my actionable steps to get clarity during trauma.

1. Seek God

Why It Matters:

Sitting in God's presence, in His stillness, and allowing peace to flood your mind dispels despair and loneliness. You will not feel alone. Prayer is communication with God. Some people do it so eloquently in front of others; however, they may never honestly communicate with Him when alone.

Prayer is the sending and receiving of holy communication. We all know He's not Santa Claus, waiting to bring you your heart's every desire. But He is a benevolent God, who will never leave you, nor forsake you. And in getting clarity during prayer, you may find that your heart's desire is not what's going to bring you fulfillment. However, you must be willing to sit in His presence and hear Him.

Real-Life Example:

I had a friend who received a word of prophecy that she would get a house. She wanted a home; she needed a house, and she was ready. The prophetic word from a pastor was all she needed to hear. Here's where we miss God. She didn't pray about it. She didn't wait for the word to be confirmed (which is scripture). She ran out and bought the first house she was approved for. The house was a money pit. She ended up walking away from the house and not looking back. She went back to being a renter, something she never wanted to do. Just a little talk with Jesus would have slowed her down and saved her dollars and sense.

How to Apply It:

Carve out time in your day to commune with Jesus. At first, it will be hard, but persevere. It gets easier, and you'll find He is a great listener. He'll teach you to listen in return.

Learn not to be uncomfortable with silence. Many of us feel that way because we don't want to do self-examination. Our inner child can remind us of all the things we have done wrong in our lives. But communing with God and His word will remind us that we are fearfully and wonderfully made, even in the midst of our mistakes.

2. Read Your Word

Why It Matters:

The Bible states that God's word is your weapon (Ephesians 6:17). So, when we go into battle without it, we are coming against giants in our lives that we cannot win against. But with God's word, a slingshot and stones are enough!

Reading your word provides clarity of thought and wisdom in life's trials. We are charged to communicate with God through His word. Here are two scriptures that can help you with this:

Isaiah 62:6 says, "You who are His servants and by your prayers put the Lord in remembrance of His promises, keep not silence."

John 15:7 states, "If you abide in me, and my words abide in you, ask whatever you wish, and it will be done for you."

Real-Life Example:

As a new Christian, my friend was unaware that God loved her. And because she had struggled to feel loved, she often accepted less in her relationships than she should have. But finally, learning not just to attend church, but to read her word, she found scriptures that helped her understand that many of the things she was going through were already resolved in her Bible. She only had to read it and believe it.

How to Apply It:

This advice seems like a repeat, but we really do need to make time for our spiritual meal every day. We would never think it was a problem to make time to eat a meal. Yet we feel like creating time to spend in our word and in His presence, and then to commune with Him, is too much work. When the first sign of trouble comes, we pick up our phone and call someone else to pray, to assure us that things will get better.

We have failed to use our weapons to repel and rebuke the things that are coming for our peace. If a robber were coming to steal your most precious gems, you wouldn't leave your weapon in the drawer. You'd pull it out and use it. Don't leave your Bible on the shelf with its brand-new, just-bought smell. Open it and devour this food for your soul and spirit.

3. Worship God in Spirit and in Truth

Why It Matters:

Worshipping God in "spirit and truth" means engaging with Him through genuine, heartfelt devotion, guided by the truth revealed in scripture, rather than through mere ritual or Sunday church exercises. It matters because it reflects a transformed heart, a deeper connection with God, and a more meaningful expression of faith. Would you ask your father, with whom you have no relationship, to help you? No, you wouldn't. To have the kind of breakthrough I had with God in that hotel room, I had to rebuild my relationship with God.

Real-Life Example:

Initially, I was not feeling God in that hotel room. I wanted to stay where I was: miserable. (Some of us are not trying to get better.) But I had a small ember burning beneath my pain, and that ember still hungered for God. That small flame brought me to some truths I needed to move from bitterness to forgiveness.

How to Apply It:

1. Move to an Authentic Relationship:

- Worshiping in spirit emphasizes an internal, heartfelt connection with God, rather than just outward rituals or formalities.

- It's about offering your true self, with all your thoughts, emotions, and desires, to God. *Even if those thoughts are messy, God can handle them.*

2. Be Guided by Truth:

- Worshiping in truth means aligning your worship with God's revealed will and character as found in scripture. *This is where the mess starts becoming an internal message.*

- It involves understanding God's nature, His commandments, and His plan for salvation, and allowing that understanding to shape your worship.

- This includes recognizing Jesus Christ as the truth and the way to God.

3. Transformation and Growth:

- True worship, offered in spirit and truth, leads to personal transformation, making you more spiritual, loving, and Christlike.

- It allows you to experience God's presence and love more fully, and to reflect that love to others.

- Worship becomes a catalyst for spiritual growth and a more vibrant relationship with God.

4. Beyond Ritual:

- Worshiping in spirit and truth moves beyond mere outward expressions or adherence to religious traditions.

- It encompasses all aspects of life, as every action can be an offering to God when done with a heart of worship.

- This includes work, relationships, and even everyday tasks, all done in a way that honors God.

5. God's Desire:

- God desires genuine, heartfelt worship aligned with His truth.

- He seeks a relationship with His people that is based on love, trust, and obedience.

- Worship in spirit and truth is a response to God's grace and a way to express our love and devotion to Him.

There is a sentence in the marriage vows that reads, "What God has put together, let no man separate," which conveys the idea that marriage, ordained by God, is a sacred and permanent union. It's rooted in biblical teachings and emphasizes the sanctity and lifelong commitment of marriage. The phrase, often spoken by Jesus in the Gospels, highlights that when a couple enters into marriage, God unites them, and this union is meant to be unbroken. But we understand that in our divinity, we are human. We fail to live up to what has been handed down to us in a sacred manner. Yet, we serve a forgiving God, who mends broken pieces as a mission. We only need to enter His presence to find our way home.

Prayer Break

Lord, when we are in a place of betrayal, hurt, and anger,
be our refuge, as promised in Psalm 91.
Remind us that marriage is Your covenant,
designed to anchor us in what You have purposed.

Grant us a Selah moment before we act.
May we dwell in Your secret place—
choosing pause over panic,
and wisdom over reaction.

Amen.

Chapter 4

Greg A Year of Consequences

That year after our divorce was the longest year of my life. Dog years, if you want to really understand my journey. I didn't just sit in the mess I made; I stewed. I had to face the pain, the regret, and the reality of what I had done.

Divorce statistics show that only 6 percent of divorced couples ever remarry each other.[8]

I felt that the odds of turning my life around were against me. I hadn't had a Huxtable upbringing (it turns out even the Huxtables hadn't had a Huxtable upbringing). Carolyn was my North Star, the compass that kept me straight, even though I was boundless and rebellious in our marriage. She kept me.

Now she had moved on. She was rebuilding her life without me. And I had to accept that I had lost her forever.

It was terrifying.

There comes a tiredness that doesn't just sit in your body; it seeps into your veins and runs through your organs, sapping even the thought of what appears to be energy. That's what I found myself waking up to every day: nothingness. In those days, we didn't talk about mental health crises; we didn't even breathe it. I had no measuring stick to compare to where I had been and where I was.

---

[8] The New York Times, Psychology Today

I can tell you this: I was tired of getting high. But I started getting high at the age of thirteen. It had me. It took so much effort to act as though I was okay when it was all a lie. The drugs helped me cope, but I was beginning to realize they were also a problem. There is a scripture where the Apostle Paul states, that which we hate, we do. I didn't know that scripture then, but I was living it. No matter how much dope I did, happiness eluded me. Other women only made Carolyn's absence more severe. Hanging out with friends made me lonelier. I was out of control, doing four to five Primos deep—marijuana laced with cocaine—getting dressed for work like it was just another Tuesday.

During one of our arguments, Carolyn accused me of being an addict. I was offended. Looking into a mirror, I began to question if my offense was really denial. I needed intervention, and the last one to honestly care about my soul had walked out. But God . . . God will walk into a Wendy's on South High Street wearing human skin and call it a rescue.

I knew Charles from back in the day. Grace, grace running into him at Wendy's, was a lifeline when I didn't realize I was drowning. He stood before me as we gave the universal brother handshake, looking me hard in the eye.

"Hey, man, how you doing?" Charles asked as he gripped my hand in greeting.

"I'm good. Getting me something to eat. Ain't seen you in a minute," I answered, realizing as I stood there that I hadn't seen him out in the streets.

"Right, right. Hey, slide me your number, and we can chop it up later. I've got to get going," Charles said as he held up his food.

We exchanged numbers, and as he left, he turned and said, with urgency, "Seriously, man, call me."

There was something different about Charles. A calmness, like peace, had found his address and moved in. His pupils weren't dilated. Now, the game recognizes the game, and I could no longer see his.

I did not call him. I was in a perpetual pity party, and there was no plus-one.

But God. That one sentence changes the trajectory of a momentum that is going in the wrong direction. One word, I believe, that God engineered to allow His eraser to redirect our journey.

But!

My phone rang. I looked at it, not even understanding that my hesitation to answer was the enemy's desire to sift me like wheat.

"Yeah?" I answered.

"Meet me." Just that. No thunder. No scripture. Just obedience disguised as concern.

We sat at Wendy's. My nerves were buzzing, and my heart was pounding. I kept thinking we'd talk a little, catch up, and then, after that, I'd go to work and pretend to be okay. Instead, I was confronted with my drug abuse. Truth sat in front of me and read me like yesterday's front-page news. He told me that he had fallen four times before he got up for good, but he kept trying. He knew God wanted him to live a better life. And he wanted me to know that he wanted a better life for me too.

I got up and left, not risking a change that I needed more than anything. Good change could be scary.

Now, here is where it gets good, and God shows off. I didn't know that Carolyn had run into Charles somewhere along the way, and he asked her how we were doing. She told him we were divorced, and she didn't know how I was doing. He gave her his number and told her to have me call him.

Meanwhile, I ran into him. He says nothing. But when I get home, Carolyn chooses that moment to call me, relay Charles's message, and give me his number.

God was not playing. Carolyn could have kept the number and the encounter to herself, but she called and gave it to me. I had a spark of hope. She didn't hate me. Maybe I could quit hating myself for my poor choices.

So, I called.

"Meet me," he answered.

I met him, and today, I can't tell you at what point his suggestion of taking me to the hospital's rehab unit became my yes to going. But it happened.

I remember him stating, "Greg, you don't have to stay. No one's forcing you. But your other option is to keep doing what you're doing—and die from it. I can be your sponsor, but if you're playing, don't bother me. I take this seriously."

No soft serve. No sugar.

Sometimes, the mercy of God doesn't come wrapped in comfort. Sometimes, it drives you to the psych floor and hands you a clipboard.

Charles drove me, leaving my car in Wendy's parking lot, where it stayed for thirty days. *Shout out to Wendy's.*

I checked myself in.

Walking through those doors, I made God real. *"Lord, I'm tired. Help."*

Rehab isn't for the weakhearted. It smells like bleach, brokenness, and burnt coffee. But it becomes holy ground when surrender walks through the door.

Some folks are there for mama, daddy, husband, or others. But you have to get clean for yourself.

Carolyn and I were divorced. She visited sometimes—not with promises—just with presence. And one day, a counselor asked me, *"Who is she to you?"*

"My . . . ex-wife." The words caught like barbed wire in my throat.

And that counselor, God bless him, didn't blink. He leaned in and told me the kind of truth that shifts your bones:

"Greg, don't get sober to win her back because she may never come back. And if she doesn't—you'll go right back to what tried to kill you. So, if you're going to heal, heal for you. Heal for God—or don't bother."

That was the day I stopped trying to hustle grace. They don't tell you this part—but I will.

When the drugs leave your body, the memories come back. The silence gets loud. Your sins line up like unpaid bills—and depression pulls up a chair.

I didn't want to get high anymore. I wanted my life back. I wanted the woman I'd broken. I wanted forgiveness without paying the cost. I desired the lethargic feeling of walking through water to leave my body. I didn't know depression had taken up residence. I was ignorant. All I had ever heard from Christians was that God could fix it.

Fix me, Jesus.

But God isn't a vending machine. And healing—*real* healing—ain't buy-one-get-one-free with marriage and joy on the side.

Carolyn ignored me in public like I was smoke. My family told me to move on. I tried dating someone else. But everything felt counterfeit—like trying to wear another man's skin.

That's when depression showed up. Not loud. Not dramatic. Just steady. The kind that lies on your chest in the morning and whispers, *"Why try?"*

I did my thirty days and got sober. It didn't bring Carolyn back.

Jesus, where is my reward?

And depression was consistently knocking on my door. It kept saying, "I'm here."

I wasn't in church yet. My Bible was still dusty. But I was getting desperate, and I knew how to talk.

So, I started talking to God.

Not fancy prayers, where the person runs out of air as he breathes deeply, shouting and working up a sweat. Not the "most gracious Heavenly Father" kind.

I prayed the way broken men pray:

"God . . . Take this taste out of my mouth."

"God . . . I can't do this sober."

"God . . . If you're real, don't let me die like this."

Sometimes, I sat in a dark room. Sometimes, I drove across the city with no music—just me and God riding in silence until I cried or felt peace. I didn't know it yet, but those drives became altars.

Life kept moving.

One day, at a Jazz Festival in Cincinnati, Ohio, with thousands of people and amidst that noise and light . . . I saw Carolyn.

And she saw me.

I was standing there with another woman. Carolyn looked like healing in human form. And just like that, old habits arose, stinkin', thinkin' in a sober body. My missing her came back like a fever.

Wanting her, needing her.

The next morning, my phone rang. "You don't know what I want."

"I don't," I said, "but I've got a feeling you're gonna tell me."

It was Carolyn. Not yelling and not accusing of old wounds.

She said, *"Would you like to come talk?"*

I had already found out where she lived—call it hope or obsession. But that day, she laid out the rules. If we were going to talk, there would be truth, and boundaries, and no miracles on demand.

And I said yes. Because when you've been to the bottom, a boundary feels like a blessing.

Right there, in that quiet room, I made another vow—no tuxedo, no preacher, no rings:

"Lord, if you give me another chance with her, I won't waste it."

A sense of rightness fell over me, and I truly surrendered to God. I didn't just ask for help, I *begged* for it. I had gone to rehab. I'd gotten clean. I'd sought counseling. I repented not just to Carolyn but to God, to my family, and to myself. You can't just talk about change; you have to embrace it. And it takes an abundance of difficult, soul-searching work.

Slowly, I began to evolve not just on the outside, but on the inside. I became a man who wanted to be better, not just for myself, but for the people I had hurt. I wanted to prove that I could be a man of integrity, a man of faith, a man who could be trusted again.

Then something unexpected happened: that conversation began, and slowly but surely, Carolyn started talking to me again. At first, it was small things. Conversations about her boys. Checking in. Then, over time, something shifted.

At the time, I believed she saw the man I was becoming, not the man I had been. However, in retrospect, I now realize she was on her own journey of discovery and was seeing me through her own evolved eyes. She could see the new me. The one who was not only drug-free but also repentant. It took time. It took patience. It took faith. But one day, Carolyn made a choice that I will never stop being grateful for . . . She remarried me.

Let *that* sink in: the woman I had brought so much confusion, pain, and dysfunction to our sacred vows, the woman I lost, chose to love me again.

That's not just love. That's grace.

The power of redemption is incredible. When I tell people our story, they don't believe it. They say, "Most women wouldn't take a man back after that." And they're right. Most wouldn't. But Carolyn is not like most women. She is a woman of God, a woman of strength, a woman who believes in redemption.

Our story is proof that God can restore what is broken, against all the odds. Others have done it, too. But staying together is only a small part of the equation of a successful reconciliation.

A strong statistic regarding reconciliation after infidelity is that **between 60% and 75% of couples choose to stay together**

after an affair is discovered, according to several clinical studies and surveys.

Prognosis improves significantly for couples who commit to professional help. Research consistently shows that 60% to 80% of couples who attend specialized infidelity counseling are able to rebuild their relationships, often reporting the relationship to be stronger afterward than before the affair.[9]

One notable study (Atkins et al., 2012) found that couples who disclosed the affair and actively addressed it in therapy had a 57% chance of remaining together five years later, whereas only 20% of couples where the affair remained secret stayed together over the same period.[10]

We weren't halfway through creating a harmonious home.

***

I held a government job, and by God's grace, I had it until I retired. I bought my first house in my twenties. People didn't know about my vices and turmoil because I hid them. My sins were undercover, like many of yours. I just appeared young and prosperous. But in telling my story, I have chosen to be transparent because I need you to understand that a man can change. Anyone

---

9 AffairHealing.com Infidelity in U.S. Marriages. Prevalence vs Impact July 20, 2025 https://www.affairhealing.com/blog/marriage-infidelity-stats#:~:text=Reconciliation%20After%20Infidelity,in%20divorce%20following%20an%20infidelity.
10 Atkins, D. C., Marín, R. Á., Lo, T. T. Y., & Christensen, A. (2012). Relationship outcomes over 5 years following therapy. Couple and Family Psychology: Research and Practice, 1(4), 212–223. The full article can often be accessed via the American Psychological Association (APA) PsycNet or PubMed platforms

telling you he can't is a liar. But it takes making a decision, a living God, and doing the work.

When God is at the center, anything is possible.

Carolyn didn't take me back because it was easy. She took me back because she believed in the power of change, forgiveness, and love.

Betrayal almost destroyed us. But love—real, godly (agape) love—saved us.

I don't deserve Carolyn's forgiveness (none of us deserves God's forgiveness), but I will spend the rest of my life proving that I am worthy of the second chance she gave me. I'm not resting on His grace; I'm exercising His redemption.

Now, for station identification, to keep you out of *Rebecca of Sunnybrook Farms*' fairyland, our marriage is not perfect. Some scars may never fully fade. But today, we are stronger than we ever were before.

If there's one thing I've learned, it's this: God's grace is greater than our worst mistakes.

Betrayal was a chapter in our story, but it was not the final chapter. Love won. And for that, I will forever be grateful.

***

Actionable Tip: Radical Transparency

Choosing Complete Honesty to Restore Trust

Rebuilding after betrayal isn't easy. Trust is like glass; once broken, it may never look the same, but with care, intentionality, and faith, it can be repaired. Radical transparency is one of the most powerful ways to begin that process. It requires being completely open, honest, and accountable to your spouse in every area of life, removing secrecy so love can grow in its place.

Why It Matters:

After betrayal, small seeds of doubt are sown. Without transparency, those seeds multiply, threatening to choke out the relationship. Being radically transparent eliminates secrecy, fosters safety, and demonstrates to your spouse that they are seen, heard, and valued.

Real-Life Example:
The Weekly Marriage Check-In:

A couple I know who survived infidelity created a weekly marriage check-in. Every Sunday night, they sat down for a transparent, judgment-free conversation. They asked three questions:

1. How are we doing as a couple this week?

2. Is there anything that made you feel uncomfortable or uneasy in our relationship?

3. What can I do better to make you feel loved and secure?

4. At first, these talks were uncomfortable, but over time, they became a powerful tool for rebuilding trust. The betrayed spouse had a safe space to express concerns, and the other spouse stayed accountable in their journey of change.

How to Apply It:

- Give your spouse complete access to your phone, email, and social media—no hidden messages, no secret conversations.

- Be honest about your struggles. If you're feeling tempted, talk about it before it becomes a problem.

- Set up regular check-ins where you ask, *"Is there anything I'm doing that makes you feel unsafe or unsure about us?"*

Why It Works:

- It eliminates secrecy and keeps communication open.

- Minor issues are addressed before they grow into bigger problems.

- The betrayed spouse feels valued, secure, and respected.

Place Faith At The Center

Why It Matters:

Even the best tools will fail without the willingness to believe in healing. Faith that God can restore what's broken, faith that love—when it is real—can survive deep wounds, and faith that actual change is possible are the cornerstones of lasting restoration.

Real-Life Example:

Our Story:

Betrayal took us to the edge of destruction. But love brought us back. Our story is not one of a perfectionist's story of pain, loss, redemption, and grace. Today, I can say without hesitation: Carolyn is not just my wife; she is my hero.

How to Apply It:
I was a liar who had to embrace the truth.

When couples embrace radical transparency, they choose courage over comfort and truth over pretense. It's not about dwelling on the past; it's about creating a future where trust can breathe again. With intentional action, daily commitment, and faith in God's healing, a stronger, healthier marriage is possible.

Gregory L. Napier & Carolyn L Napier

49

CONTINUING THE WORK

Prayer Break

Lord, You have taught us that faith without works is dead.
As we move through these chapters,
help us recognize Your work in the Spirit,
even when progress is not yet visible in the natural.

With mustard-seed faith, we endure.
We trust the process, Lord,
and we trust You.

Amen.

Chapter 5

The Unpacking of the Baggage in a Marriage

Carolyn sifted through the mail, looking for the overdue check that was two days old. She couldn't understand why she hadn't received it. She was determined that when she got to work, she would give someone a nudge to get the check to her as promised. She had already earmarked that money for some things that needed to be taken care of, and she wasn't sure why, but she felt anxious about the delay.

"Honey, I'm leaving for work now," Greg said as he grabbed his coffee and sauntered to the door.

He left a lot earlier than she did, so Carolyn held out her cheek for his usual peck and murmured, "Okay, have a good day."

She then bit her lip as she laid the mail down with a sigh.

Greg had been in a good mood for the last few days, the direct opposite of her anxiety. But she was glad that at least one of them was feeling good.

Shaking off a feeling of apprehension, she headed into the office.

Carolyn's position as an HR manager had its positive side, and one of them was being able to expedite a trace on the check that she should have received. Now, she just had to wait for news.

The next day, checking after work and not receiving her check again, Carolyn rushed into the office for some answers.

Her office assistant hesitantly entered her office. "Ms. Carolyn, I received the trace on your check; it was cashed. I have a copy of the cancelled check here."

She handed Carolyn the check and then awkwardly left.

Carolyn's face stilled as she flipped the check over and saw her name sprawled in Greg's writing.

What has he done?

***

Marriage is often portrayed by society as being about love, laughter, and a lifetime of togetherness. Girls in pigtails dream of white flowing dresses, a handsome prince to whisk them away to their adorable house and its white picket fence. Young boys imagine being the king of their castles, waited on by the fair damsels they rescue, and bringing home the bacon, where she swoons at his manliness. Nobody prepares young people for the reality of compromise, the need to communicate, and the financial stability and skills required to run a family.

These societal misconceptions rarely prepare two people who bring their past hurts, habits, and beliefs into their shared home. Each person has a journey, and everyone carries baggage along the way. Looking inside our baggage reveals our backgrounds, issues, experiences, personality traits, parenting, emotional intelligence, and coping skills. Some bags are light and easy to set down, while others are so overstuffed that we can barely close the zipper. We drag them because they become too heavy to lift. Over time, dragging causes fraying, which can lead to the contents spilling out at inconvenient moments.

Carolyn and I had no idea how much baggage we were carrying until we were forced to face it. The first few months of marriage were wonderful. We were excited about the future, but soon, our past started creeping in. The contents of our bags begin spilling out. In our haste to hide our soiled linen, we started throwing things back inside, not wanting to communicate our vulnerabilities. But the bag is frayed, no longer equipped to handle what was once a simple task: hiding your belongings not just from the world, but also from your spouse.

Small arguments grew into major fights. Minor misunderstandings escalated into sharp words. It felt like we were living with ghosts, memories, fears, and expectations that didn't belong to our marriage but were influencing how we treated each other. We needed to start unpacking, but we needed to do it intentionally.

One of the most significant issues we faced was a lack of trust. The above anecdote about me cashing Carolyn's check was from our first marriage. During that time, I had spent years struggling with addiction, and even though I was now clean, Carolyn still carried the fear that I would fall back into old patterns. I had broken her trust in so many different ways, in various situations, that she was still experiencing the aftershocks of our destructive history. She needed to know that her demand for my transparency in all matters would not make me leave. And I needed to prepare myself to give her what she needed without resenting the circumstances. She had once unquestioningly trusted me; now I had to help her believe in me again.

Her past had taught her that relationships fall apart when things get hard, so she built walls to protect herself. Meanwhile, I had learned to survive on my own, which made it hard for me to truly depend on someone else being there for me. Our marriage was not just about two people; it was about two histories coming together to create one future.

We had differing views on how to handle problems. Carolyn believed in talking it through, but I had always been someone who avoided conflict. When she wanted to discuss something, I shut down. To her, that felt like rejection. I felt overwhelmed and wanted space. The more we ignored these differences, the more resentment grew.

One night, after another argument, Carolyn finally said, "I don't know how to do this if we don't face what we're bringing into this marriage." Her words hit me hard. She was right. We were still carrying wounds from the past, but we hadn't made space for healing.

That night, we made a conscious decision to be honest about our baggage and work through it as a couple.

Our first step was to have a "baggage talk." We set aside time each week to talk about the baggage we brought into our marriage. We each picked one issue at a time—trust, communication, and childhood experiences—and discussed where our beliefs originated. Instead of blaming each other, we listened.

We asked, "How can we, together, make this work?" The goal wasn't to fix everything in one night, but to understand and support each other. And as we addressed each issue, it came out of the bag and was hung up in clear view of both of us, no longer hidden.

If baggage is weighing on your marriage, don't ignore it. Set a time, sit down, and start unpacking—together. Even airlines penalize you if your baggage exceeds the allowed weight. Avoid a crash landing in your marriage . . . unpack.

***

Unpacking

Every couple brings history into their relationship—memories, habits, fears, and expectations formed long before "I do." This baggage doesn't just vanish when the wedding vows are spoken; it lingers in the background, shaping how we communicate, react, and love. If left unaddressed, these hidden issues can become obstacles, turning minor disagreements into major divides. The good news? Baggage can be unpacked, and when it is, couples create space for healing and trust to develop.

1. Identify and Acknowledge Your Baggage

Why It Matters:

You can't heal from what you won't face. Many couples try to hide their past wounds, thinking they can overcome them without ever acknowledging them. But unspoken pain will always find a way to spill out, usually at the worst possible moment. Acknowledging your baggage doesn't weaken your marriage; it strengthens it by making sure you're fighting the problem, *not* each other.

Real-Life Example:

The Baggage Talks:

When Carolyn and I realized our past was leaking into our present, we began setting aside time each week to unpack it together. Sometimes, that meant revisiting painful moments from our first marriage—like when I cashed her check without her knowing—so we could talk openly about the mistrust it caused. We didn't try to solve everything at once. We simply named what was in the bag, laid it out in the open, and let each other see it without judgment.

How to Apply It:

Set aside intentional time for a "baggage talk" each week.

Choose one area—trust, communication, past relationships, finances—and share where your beliefs and behaviors came from.

Listen without interrupting or defending. The goal is understanding, not fixing, at that moment.

2. Commit to Carrying It Together

Why It Matters:

Baggage feels lighter when it's shared. When each spouse tries to carry their past alone, isolation grows and connection weakens. But when you commit to carrying the weight together, it turns into an opportunity for deeper trust and unity.

Real-Life Example:
From Isolation to Unity:

Early in our remarriage, Carolyn feared that my old habits would return, and I wrestled with letting someone in. We realized that trust would only grow if we faced those fears together as a team. That meant me giving her transparency without resentment, and her giving me space without assuming the worst. Each time we worked through an old wound together, our bond grew stronger.

How to Apply It:

- Replace blame with empathy. Remember, the past shaped both of you.

- Ask regularly, *"How can I help you carry this?"* and be prepared to listen to the answer.

- Celebrate progress, even if it's small—every step toward understanding matters.

Closing Reflection:

Ignoring baggage in marriage is like boarding a plane with an overloaded suitcase—it might make it onto the flight, but eventually, something will burst open. The most loving thing you can do for your marriage is to unpack what's inside, name it, and decide together how to carry it. When we made that choice, our home shifted from a battleground of unspoken hurts to a place where love, understanding, and grace could finally breathe.

Chapter 5 :
Unpacking Your Baggage – Worksheet

Reflection: What baggage are you carrying?

Think about past hurts, fears, or habits that still affect your marriage today. Write them down here:

Worksheet Questions – Check the correct answer

1. Why is it essential to identify and acknowledge your baggage in marriage?

   a) Because it weakens the relationship

   b) Because unspoken pain will spill out eventually

   c) Because it gives you a reason to blame your spouse

   d) Because it makes arguments more exciting

2. What is the goal of a "baggage talk"?

   a) To fix everything in one night

   b) To judge each other's past

   c) To understand, not to fix immediately

   d) To avoid discussing uncomfortable issues

3. How does committing to carry baggage together help a marriage?

   a) It isolates each spouse so they can deal with it alone

   b) It creates opportunities for blame

   c) It lightens the load and builds unity

   d) It keeps problems hidden

4. What's a practical way to carry baggage together?

    a) Ask regularly, "How can I help you carry this?"

    b) Ignore your spouse's past

    c) Expect your spouse to fix everything alone

    d) Pretend the baggage doesn't exist

Action Steps

Schedule a "baggage talk" this week. What topic will you start with?

____

____

____

List one way you can support your spouse in carrying their baggage:

____

____

____

Closing Reflection

Ignoring baggage is like boarding a plane with an overloaded suitcase—it will eventually burst open.

Reflect on one piece of baggage you and your spouse can unpack together this month:

____

____

To download or use the fillable online worksheet, please go to our Married With A Purpose website: ttvttg.com

Chapter 6

Unequally Yoked

Faith is supposed to bring people together. But in our marriage, it was a dividing line. I had a relationship with God. I knew His power, His love, and His ability to change lives. But Greg? He wasn't there yet. He respected my faith, but he didn't share it in the same way.

We had overcome so much. Greg's addiction. His deceitfulness. We were beginning to see our way clear. But being unequally yoked was an issue we had not overcome. At first, I thought it wouldn't matter. I thought my faith would be enough for both of us. However, over time, the difference became increasingly apparent. As a Christian, we approach life differently (or should) than non-Christians.

I wanted to pray about decisions. Greg made his choices based on logic. I wanted to trust God with our finances. He wanted to be in complete control. I wanted to go to church as a family on Sundays. Greg saw it as just another day with the bonus of all-day football.

The hardest part? After a while, I began to feel alone in my faith.

There were nights when I prayed for our marriage, hoping God would move in Greg's heart. There were days when I wanted to talk about what God was teaching me, but I wasn't sure Greg would understand.

Being married to someone who didn't share my faith was one of the loneliest experiences of my life. I had no idea how other couples managed to do it.

Women had outpaced men in church attendance since 2000, at 47 percent to 38 percent, before men began outpacing women in 2022, at 35 percent to 30 percent. In 2024, 30 percent of men were attending weekly compared to 27 percent of women. The majority of men attending church are married.[11]

Carolyn

It had been a long week at work, and my Saturday had been errand-filled. We were now living in Pittsburgh, PA, but I was a member of a church in Columbus, Ohio. And I knew that the next day, I would be making that trip alone. But I kept trying to get Greg to join me.

I entered the kitchen where he was pouring a glass of iced tea. I slowly approached him, silently repeating to myself not to be heavy-handed, but to give him one more opportunity to join me at the Lord's house the next day.

"You want a glass?" he asked as I approached.

I shook my head and eased into a chair at the kitchen table. Smiling, he sat next to me and took a sip.

Swallowing, with hope, I asked, "Would you like to attend church with me tomorrow?"

The smile on Greg's face wavered and then reappeared. "No, Carolyn. I'm going to put my feet up and watch the game."

I rose, and a little dejected, I went to our bedroom to prepare for bed. Looking around for my purse, I realized I had left it in the car. It

---

[11] Barna Group (data analyzed by Daniel Copeland, VP of Research), "New Research: Men vs Women at Church," Barna Group, Accessed 2025. https://www.barna.com/trends/church-attendance-women-men/

had been that kind of day. I got up and went outside. Climbing into the car, I leaned over from the driver's side and picked up my purse.

A powerful wave of the Holy Spirit filled the car, and my eyes welled with tears. I so wanted my husband to know this feeling. The voice of my prayers filled the car, and I prayed for Greg, our marriage, and our walk with God, leaving me overwhelmed with hope. I wanted this marriage, which was mending daily, to be founded in Christ.

Greg

I placed my tea on the table and watched as Carolyn walked away. Her shoulders were a little lower than before, her gait less buoyant. I loved my wife, but as we progressed in our renewed marriage walk, we had promised to be honest in all things. And I wasn't feeling like church was a necessary part of my life. But maybe I could talk to her one more time and convince her to let this go once and for all.

I walked across our hallway, and glancing out the window, I saw Carolyn sitting in the car.

Wondering what was going on, I went outside and could hear her on the phone. Approaching, I found it wasn't a phone call she was on, but a call to God.

Overhearing her fervent prayer became the turning point.

"Lord, how do I do this? How do I love someone who doesn't see you the way I do?"

Carolyn's sincere cry stopped me in my tracks. I *felt* it.

Carolyn

The answer to my prayer came, not in a loud voice, but in a whispered truth.

Twice The Vows Twice The Grace

Love him where he is.

Not where I wanted him to be. Not where I expected him to be. Or where I was. That changed everything. Instead of forcing faith on him, I started living it out. Instead of arguing about God, I showed him His love through my actions. Instead of trying to change him, I prayed for God to work in His own time.

***

There are other ways to become unequally yoked. Maybe you began your spiritual walk together. And then something slowed in one of you, almost to a stop.

Meet Daryl and Monique Harrison. Married twelve years, faithful churchgoers, and once passionate about building a life grounded in Christ. But somewhere between soccer practice and promotions, Daryl stopped praying. And Monique stopped dreaming.

She noticed first. He didn't want to do devotions anymore. She'd talk about her women's ministry; he'd nod, distracted by his phone.

Her being her, she asked, "Are you listening? Why are you acting so distant? Don't you care anymore? Believe?"

He said, "I believe, babe . . . I just don't feel the need to prove it every day."

"I'm not asking you to prove it. I'm asking you to *pursue it.*"

And that's when it hit her: *they were spiritually unequally yoked,* even though they shared a last name, a mortgage, and matching Bible covers.

Why It Matters:

Becoming Unequally Yoked After Marriage

- 2 Corinthians 6:14 tells us not to be unequally yoked—but what happens when that yoke *slips midjourney?*

- One spouse stops growing, and suddenly, the burden shifts. One is dragging, the other is straining.

- But hear this: spiritual stagnation *isn't final.* It's a *signal.*

Remember: Stagnant water stinks—not because it's dead, but because it's not moving.

Real-Life Example:

Darryl and Monique were struggling. They were no longer moving together, and one of them didn't seem to care that they were out of step.

How to Apply It:

Our Acronym Today is: R.E.V.I.V.E.

To help you rekindle your connection when your marriage feels stuck.

- R – Recognize the Stagnation: Denial delays healing. Acknowledge the spiritual gap.

- E – Extend Grace, Not Guilt: Shaming your spouse into growth is not biblical love.

- V – Verbally Invite Growth: Gently open up conversations. Ask: "Can we pray together?" or "What's God showing you this week?"

- I – Initiate the Flow: Go first. Attend the study. Worship fully. Grow aloud. Sometimes, fire spreads.

- V – Value the Small Wins: Celebrate spiritual steps, not leaps.

- E – Entrust the Outcome to God: Growth is God's work. Your job is to stay faithful, not forceful.

How Do You Restore the Fire?

1. Pray *for* your spouse, not *about* them. There's a difference.

2. Fast for clarity—not control. Let God show you if you're enabling comfort or encouraging growth.

3. Counseling is not a defeat. It's discipleship in disguise.

4. Go back to your first love. Not them—*Him*. Rekindling your passion for God can reignite theirs.

Remember, you don't fix stagnation by shaking the cup. You fix it by pouring in fresh water.

So, if your spouse has stopped growing, don't panic. Plant. Water. And *trust God for the increase.* As it says in 1 Corinthians 3:6—*"I planted the seed, Apollos watered it, but God has been making it grow."*

Still growing. Still learning. Still yoked. And we're praying that you continue to move forward, together. We were still learning how to walk together in faith.

This chapter has presented scenarios of two couples who are unequally yoked. I had led Carolyn to believe we could walk together in harmonious faithfulness. But even though we were now remarried, I was still not embracing the entire walk God wanted from me. The other couple had entered equal, walking together, but along the way, one fell out of sync, not only with the other but with God. REVIVE gave us a plan to restart our engines.

The common denominator in both these instances was *change.* Change is necessary at some point with everyone. But how do we manifest it when we recognize change is needed?

Modeling Change in a Marriage:

The following steps can be applied to any behavior you wish to change in your marriage. Modeling is the act of consciously or unconsciously demonstrating desired behaviors or attitudes, essentially acting as a positive example for your partner. In a marriage—especially one divided in faith—your actions can speak louder than any argument or plea.

1. Let Your Life Speak

Why It Matters:

When faith is divided, words can sometimes build walls instead of bridges. Nagging and pressure may push your spouse away, but a life lived consistently in faith becomes a silent sermon they cannot ignore. Demonstrating patience, love, and service plants seeds that, in God's timing, can grow into transformation.

Real-Life Example:
A Journey Toward Faith

Years later—yes, it took *years*—my heart softened. I saw God through Carolyn's actions, not her words. We lived in Pennsylvania, and she drove to Columbus, Ohio, every weekend to attend church. She asked me to participate with her, and I said no at first. What she didn't know was that I had begun watching Pastor Joyce Meyer on TV, even hiding it so she wouldn't press me to attend church. Weeks later, when she asked again, I said yes.

I began to enjoy attending with her. To my surprise, the pastor's sermons aligned with what I had been hearing from Joyce Meyer. I still remember the day the pastor gave an altar call. I raised my hand—just high enough to respond, yet low enough to think no one saw. Little did I know that twenty years later, I would be called to pastor.

How to Apply It:

- Don't nag or pressure—show your values through consistent action.

- Love them unconditionally, even when they don't share your beliefs.

- Serve them faithfully and be patient, trusting God to move at the right time.

2. Trust God's Timing

Why It Matters:

Real change often takes longer than we expect. Pressing for immediate results can backfire, but trusting God allows transformation to happen in His perfect timing. Faith that is chosen, not forced, is faith that lasts.

Real-Life Example:
The Long View

Carolyn modeled the benefits of being a Christian who walked by faith. She never tried to force me into belief. She lived it so consistently that I could not deny the peace and strength it brought her. When I finally chose salvation, it was because God had drawn me—*not* because I had been pushed. That choice became the foundation for the life and ministry we share today.

How to Apply It:

- Release control—allow God to work in your spouse's heart.

- Celebrate small signs of openness, even if they seem insignificant.

- Remain faithful in your walk, even if you see no immediate change.

Closing Reflection:

Modeling is more than behavior; it's ministry in motion. It's living in such a way that your marriage becomes a testimony of grace, patience, and God's power to change hearts. When words fail, your life can still speak—and sometimes, it's the quiet witness that brings the loudest transformation.

> **Listen to Podcast #39 On Apple or Spotify: Why Your Marriage Isn't Growing/Stop Trying to Be the Holy Spirit: Build a Christ-Centered Marriage When You're in Different Spiritual Seasons**
>
> **Link:** https://why-your-marriage-isnt-growing.captivate.fm/

Chapter 6:
Unequally Yoked – Worksheet

Reflection:
Unequally Yoked in Marriage

Have you ever felt spiritually out of sync with your spouse? Write about a moment when your faith practices or beliefs felt different:

____

____

____

____

____

____

Worksheet Questions – Check the correct answer

1. What does it mean to be "unequally yoked" in marriage?

    a) One spouse earns more money than the other

    b) One spouse has stronger or different faith practices

    c) One spouse is taller than the other

    d) One spouse works more hours

2. According to the chapter, what is the danger of being unequally yoked?

    a) It always leads to divorce

    b) It can create feelings of loneliness and division in faith

    c) It means you can't pray at all

d) It makes communication impossible

3. In the acronym R.E.V.I.V.E., what does the "E" stand for?

a) Expect Perfection

b) Extend Grace, Not Guilt

c) Emphasize Control

d) Eliminate Differences

4. What is one way to model change in a marriage?

a) Nag and pressure your spouse into church attendance

b) Live out your faith consistently through love and service

c) Argue until they agree with you

d) Keep silent and withdraw from your spouse

5. Why is trusting God's timing important in an unequally yoked marriage?

a) Because forced faith rarely lasts

b) Because it avoids responsibility

c) Because waiting requires no effort

d) Because you can ignore your spouse's needs

Action Steps

Using the R.E.V.I.V.E. framework, write one way you can encourage spiritual growth in your marriage this week:

____

____

____

How can you model faith in your marriage without pressuring your spouse?

____

____

____

Closing Reflection

Modeling faith is more than behavior—it's ministry in motion. Reflect on one way your life can speak louder than words in your marriage this month:

____

____

____

____

____

To download or use the fillable online worksheet, please go to our Married With A Purpose website: ttvttg.com

Chapter 6:
R.E.V.I.V.E. – Worksheet

Rekindling Spiritual Growth in Marriage

This workshop will guide you through each step of the R.E.V.I.V.E framework. Use this space to reflect, write, and plan how you and your spouse can grow together spiritually.

____

____

____

R – Recognize the Stagnation

Where have you noticed spiritual stagnation in your marriage? Denials delay healing—write it down here:

____

____

____

E – Extend Grace, Not Guilt

How can you show grace to your spouse without shaming them for where they are spiritually?

____

____

____

V – Verbally Invite Growth

What is one gentle question or invitation you can ask this week (e.g., "Can we pray together?" or "What's God showing you?"?

____

I – Initiate the Flow

How can you go first in pursuing growth (attend a study, worship openly, or pray aloud)?

V – Value the Small Wins

What small step of spiritual growth can you celebrate together right now?

E – Entrust the Outcome to God

What specific area do you need to release to God instead of trying to control?

Closing Reflection

R.E.V.I.V.E. is not about forcing change, but about creating space for God to move. Reflect here on how you can remain faithful while trusting God with your spouse's growth:

____

____

____

____

____

To download or use the fillable online worksheet, please go to our Married With A Purpose website: ttvttg.com

Prayer Break

Lord, we know that one of the ways we are most often unequally yoked is in our finances. Teach us to work together for the good of our families and Your Kingdom.

You remind us in Ecclesiastes 10:19
that money answers many things,
yet love, joy, peace, patience, kindness and goodness,
faithfulness, gentleness, and self-control
are spiritual fruit we receive through You. Therefore, money is a tool that we wield, and we will not allow it to control us.

Make us good stewards of what You place in our hands.
Teach us to leave an inheritance for our children,
to give generously to those less fortunate,
and to honor You in how we manage what You provide.

Amen.

Chapter 7

Handling Money as a Team

Money can be a bridge or a battleground in marriage. The statistics are sobering—41 percent of divorces are due to financial stress (Ramsey Solutions, 2023), and couples who argue about money at least once a week are 30 percent more likely to divorce than those who rarely fight about finances (National Marriage Project, 2022).[12]

Carolyn and I were no exception. We had different financial backgrounds, different spending habits, and different fears about money. She was a saver, carefully watching every dollar. I was a spender, enjoying money while I had it. At first, we brushed off our differences, thinking we could "figure it out." However, when unpaid bills began to accumulate, those differences escalated into heated arguments.

We weren't always struggling; we had stumbled into some reasonable successes over the years. Real estate and rental property, which we eventually lost. Bankruptcy. The most brutal, self-defeating thing that can happen to you is when you admit to the world that you failed.

When you look your church brethren in the face and say, "Yes, this happened." And you look at your wife and say, "I'm sorry. As the head of the house, I was obligated to keep us on task, to cover, protect, and provide for you."

---

[12] Ramsey Solutions, "The State of Personal Finance: Trends for 2023."
National Marriage Project. The State of Our Unions. Charlottesville: University of Virginia, 2022

But I was falling short of a job I took seriously.

Remarrying Carolyn came with my assurances that we would be better. But this wasn't it. And until I acknowledged the need for guidance on managing my finances, we would continue to struggle. And my knees were bruised enough from falling to pride. It was time for me to raise my hand humbly for help. I had to climb out of my hole.

However, first let me tell you that climbing out was not an overnight process. Carolyn and I were retired and on what most people consider a fixed income. I had started working a job cleaning office buildings, but while I was working, I was praying. I can't tell you how amazing it was to find out that, while you were praying for help, someone who needed help was praying too. And in your struggle, you were the answer to their prayers.

***

"Hello, Greg? Hi, this is Colette. How are you?" she said.

Colette and her husband had attended church with us for over ten years. They had recently left the church, and while still friends, it had been awhile since we had talked. She had no idea that Carolyn and I were struggling financially. As a matter of fact, the last time she had known anything about our financial situation, we had made a significant monetary donation to our church's Super Sowing Sunday. Based on that donation's size, Carolyn and I were doing well.

"I'm good. I've been missing seeing you guys at church."

She chuckled lightly. "Yes, we're missing you and Carolyn, too. And even though we're attending somewhere else, God is still good. Still answering prayers. This will sound strange, coming out of the blue, but I have a job offer for you. I know you don't need a job, but I need someone I can trust. Someone with the integrity to do the right thing even when they want to do something different personally. I've been praying for the right person, and God keeps giving me you for the job." She then haltingly asked, "Would you be interested?"

Now, I need to interject here that I *needed* a job. I needed to take some of the debt off Carolyn's and my backs. And I'd been praying. And then I got this call. I was already working a small part-time, night job cleaning offices. But the ram in the bush was braying . . .

"Wow, I am working part time. What hours are you talking about?" The whole time I'm asking, I'm praying.

"The hours are from 4:00 a.m. to 9:00 a.m. The position involves providing crisis assistance to the underserved public. Instead of having them wait outside in all kinds of weather until we open, we'd like someone outside to monitor the situation and sign people in as they drive up. This way, they can stay in their cars until we open. When we get to twenty-five families, we can let the others know to come back the next day," she said.

I laid the phone on my chest and thanked a benevolent God. She had no idea that I needed a job and that these hours were great for me. I'm an early riser, so the hours were perfect. I also found my ministry working with people who needed a word of encouragement, and the agency needed someone who could follow their rules.

I understood the director's heart; her rules weren't to hurt anyone but to ensure people stayed safe and the agency wasn't compromised. I gladly took the position. I worked there for three years. For a short period, Carolyn also worked in the office.

Diligence and perseverance equal economic freedom. After we left the company, I would tell Colette that she was the answer to my prayers. She responded, "No, *you* were an answer to mine."

Always remember that while others are playing checkers, God is playing three-dimensional chess. He doesn't add; he multiplies. It was a lesson for me that what we think He is doing for us is a way for Him to use our blessing to respond to someone else's need.

Ram meets the mountain, and the mountain is moved.

This scenario is just one peek into our past economic issues. If I showed you our history, you would be amazed at how far we've come. I could explain all day how the loss occurred, but in a nutshell, we were not moving in the same direction, and the economy was moving in a direction neither of us had anticipated. If you don't have a foundation or a spiritual blueprint for your marital financial journey, you will inevitably fail.

In the prophets of Zerubbabel, the people of Judah were tasked with rebuilding the temple, God's house, beginning with the wall. But the wall was attacked, and the plan to rebuild was not without mishaps. The people were becoming discouraged. Haggai delivered a message to the people alongside Zerubbabel. He gave them an analogy: They were like a man who worked hard but had holes in his pockets. It wasn't that money wasn't coming in, but because of the holes in his pockets (or purse), the money didn't stay. They had misplaced priorities, putting other things before their purpose of rebuilding the house.

We were at cross purposes. To move forward beyond simply replacing money, we needed to understand our shared vision as a couple to flourish. Otherwise, we were putting money in purses with holes in them.

I'll never forget the evening that changed everything. It was our breaking point. Carolyn was at the kitchen table, going over our bills. She looked at me and said, "Greg, I feel like I'm the only one worrying about money."

Her voice wasn't angry; it was tired. Defeated.

That hit me hard. She wasn't trying to control me; she was scared. Her past experiences had taught her to prepare for the worst. My past had taught me to live for today because tomorrow wasn't promised. We were both operating out of fear, but in opposite ways.

Our tension over money began to spill over into other areas of our marriage. Minor disagreements became bigger. Conversations became more stressful. Even our intimacy was affected, because, let me tell you, when financial stress is high, the emotional and physical connection suffers too.

That night, after one of our biggest arguments, we sat down and made a decision that saved our marriage: Money would not control us. We would control it.

***

Money can either be a weapon that wounds a marriage or a tool that builds it. For years, it was a weapon in our hands. We were on opposite teams—each protecting our corner—until we realized the enemy wasn't each other; it was the financial chaos that was taking over our home.

Our turning point came when we made a *Money Agreement*. That night, we stopped fighting each other and started fighting together. It was a simple, clear plan that aligned us as partners in our finances and our future.

1. Create a Money Agreement Together

Why It Matters:

Research cited by CNBC suggests that couples with differing financial perspectives are more prone to conflict and distrust. Couples with frequent financial disagreements are twice as likely to separate compared to those who are financially aligned.[13]

- More than 50 percent admit to *financial infidelity*—hiding purchases, secret bank accounts, or undisclosed debt.

- Money stress can impact mental health, leading to anxiety, depression, and increased relational conflicts.

Financial unity is not just about numbers—it's about building trust, security, and peace of mind in your marriage.

Real-Life Example:
The Night It Changed

We sat at the kitchen table with pens and paper, determined to stop the fights. Our Money Agreement covered:

1. **Budgeting:** A plan we could both live with.

2. **Redefining Money:** It belonged to *us*.

3. **Transparency:** No more secrets.

4. **Priorities:** Giving first, saving second, and a "fun money" allowance so we didn't feel deprived.

This single money agreement turned money from a source of division into a tool for building our future together.

---

[13] CNBC, "Most Couples Financially Incompatible: Having a Money Talk Could Help." February 14, 2023

How to Apply It:

- Build a budget you can *both* live with, focusing on shared goals instead of individual preferences.

- List all bills, debts, and spending habits—without judgment.

- Agree that money is *ours*—no "yours" or "mine."

- Commit to monthly money reviews—no more hidden spending or surprises.

2. Establish a Needs vs. Wants Budget

Why It Matters:

Most couples don't budget because they think it's restrictive—but a budget is freedom. It tells your money where to go, instead of leaving you wondering where it went. Dividing expenses into *needs*, *wants*, and *giving/saving* keeps spending in check while allowing room for generosity and joy.

Real-Life Example:

Carolyn and I had different ideas about what was necessary and what was not. I liked thinking big and then going after it. Carolyn was a "one step at a time, then examine the step," person. To be successful, we were going to have to learn to hear each other and do what's best for us as a family, not as individuals. Here's an important caveat: Remember that your spouse wants the best for you. There is no arbitrariness; listen and learn. You can then come to an agreement that you both can live with if you don't go into the discussion (not argument) with your mind made up. Writing it down does make it plain.

How to Apply It:

Category	Percent of Income ($5,000 a month)	Monthly Cost	Notes
Needs (Rent/Mortgage, Utilities, Groceries, Debt Payments, Insurance)	50 %	$2,500	Cover essentials first—housing, food, transportation, insurance, minimum debt payments.
Wants (Dining Out, Entertainment, Vacations, Hobbies)	30 %	$1,500	Keeps life fun and enjoyable—decide what matters most together.
Saving & Giving (Emergency Fund, Retirement, Tithing, Investments)	20 %	$1,000	Give first, save second, spend last. Build your financial future while honoring generosity.

If you're in debt, temporarily shift "wants" spending to debt payoff. If you have no emergency fund, start with $1,000 and build up to three to six months of living expenses.

3. Keep Financial Transparency and Checkpoints

Why It Matters:

Even the best financial plan will fail if it's ignored. Checkpoints keep couples accountable, prevent misunderstandings, and allow you to adjust as life changes.

Real-Life Example:
Fighting the Problem, Not Each Other:

We still have moments when we disagree about money, but now we address the *issue rather than attacking* each other. Our weekly check-ins catch problems early. Our annual vision meetings give us something to look forward to—reminding us that we're building something together.

How to Apply It:

- **Weekly Money Meeting:** Spend ten to fifteen minutes reviewing spending and upcoming bills.

- **Monthly Budget Review:** Adjust categories and priorities as needed.

- **Annual Financial Vision Meeting:** Dream together—set goals for the year, whether it's paying off debt, saving for a vacation, or investing.

Closing Reflection:

If money is a constant source of stress in your marriage, don't wait until it becomes a wall between you—take action now. Schedule a money conversation with your spouse this week. Ask, *"What's one thing we can improve financially this month?"* Create a simple budget, review it regularly, and fight for your financial future as a team.

Handled with unity, discipline, and generosity, money can be one of your greatest tools for building the marriage and the life you both deserve.

***

You may have noticed that this financial chapter was one of the longest in the book. You already understand why: Unresolved financial issues are among the biggest destroyers of marriages. Every marriage is different; maybe you're looking at the budget plan above and don't find that it works for your family. Carolyn and I, as not only marriage but also financial coaches, want to share additional budgets and their origins as possible options. We're not trying to control how you budget. We want you to know that budgeting is essential for a healthy financial portfolio, and that it's not optional if you plan to succeed.

Which Budget Method?

The "50 percent Needs/30 percent Wants/20 percent Savings" rule (as we previously illustrated) remains one of the most widely referenced budgeting frameworks today. It's straightforward, easy to understand, and has been endorsed by multiple sources:

Investopedia highlights it as a user-friendly guiding principle, ideal for covering essentials, saving, and lifestyle flexibility. NerdWallet similarly recommends this structure as a solid starting template.[14] However, for some, this may have its limitations:Time.com recommends a 60/30/10 split—especially useful in high-cost-of-living areas—allocating more to necessities and less to savings initially.[15] John Hancock warns that for many

---

[14] Investopedia, "The 50/30/20 Budget Rule Explained." NerdWallet, "The 50/30/20 Rule,"

[15] Time Magazine, "Why a 60/30/10 Budget Could Be the New 50/30/20,"

households, especially those with high expenses such as rent, child care, or health care, staying under 50 percent for needs is often impractical.[16]

So, while the 50/30/20 rule remains valid, it's best viewed as a flexible *starting point*, adjustable to real-life contexts and goals.

Christian-Focused Budgets

There are budget models designed with faith and stewardship in mind. These models intentionally *integrate faithful stewardship* and intentional giving as foundational, not optional.

FaithWorks Financial proposes a layout of 45 percent Needs/25 percent Wants/20 percent Savings, with an additional 10 percent dedicated to tithing.[17] WealthBuilders.org offers a 70 percent Expenses/20 percent Investing/10 percent Tithing model.[18] They also suggest an 80/10/10 setup for those getting started. Dave Ramsey-style Budgeting recommends detailed category percentages—for example: Giving 10 percent, Savings 10 percent, Housing 25 percent, etc.[19] A Christian Credit Union suggests at least 10 percent for generosity, followed by 12–15 percent toward savings and investing, with emergency fund development emphasized first.[20]

Which Budget?

---

[16] John Hancock, "How to Find the Right Budget Plan,"
[17] FaithWorks Financial, "Use This Christian Budget to Win at Managing Money,"

[18] WealthBuilders.org, "Understanding the 70/20/10 Budgeting Model,"
[19] Ramsey Solutions, "The State of Personal Finance: Trends for 2023
[20] AdelFi (Evangelical Christian Credit Union), "About Us." Christian Community Credit Union

- The 50/30/20 rule remains a solid, practical foundation—especially for couples starting to build financial unity.[21]

- However, it should always be tailored to your actual living costs, financial obligations, and values

- For faith-driven couples, consider incorporating tithing up front (e.g., the 45/25/20 + 10 percent model) so that your budget aligns with Christian values from the start.[22]

Suggested Table
(Updated for Christian Marriages)

Here's an adjusted version of the Needs vs. Wants table that includes tithing reflecting both practicality and faith[23]:

Category	Percent of Income	Example (Based on $5,000/Month)	Notes
Tithing Generosity	10 %	$500	Honoring faith through giving first.
Needs (Essentials)	45–50 %	$2,250–2,500	Housing, groceries, utilities, insurance, and debt payments.
Wants (Discretionary)	20–25 %	$1,000–1,250	Entertainment, dining out, hobbies.

---

[21] Investopedia, "The 50/30/20 Budget Rule Explained." NerdWallet, "The 50/30/20 Rule,"

[22] FaithWorks Financial, "Use This Christian Budget to Win at Managing Money,"

[23] FaithWorks Financial, "Use This Christian Budget to Win at Managing Money,"

Category	Percent of Income	Example (Based on $5,000/Month)	Notes
Savings/Investing	15–20 %	$750–1,000	Emergency fund, retirement, debt payoff.

Why This Works:

- Reflects Christian stewardship by prioritizing giving.

- Allows flexibility—if your needs exceed the typical 50 percent, the budget can shift accordingly.

- Encourages disciplined saving while providing room for healthy enjoyment.

Chapter 7:
Money Agreement - Worksheet

Reflect together:
What stood out to you most about our Money Agreement?

____

____

____

Needs vs. Wants

Example	Needs	Wants
	Mortgage/Rent	Designer Clothes

Budget Planning

Category	Planned Amount	Actual Amount
Tithes/Charity		
Mortgage/Rent		
Utilities		
Groceries		
Savings		
Debt Payments		
Other		

Goal-Setting Prompts

In three months, we want to:

____

____

____

In twelve months, we will:

____

____

____

Pray & Plan Space:

____

____

____

____

____

____

To download or use the fillable online worksheet, please go to our Married With A Purpose website: ttvttg.com

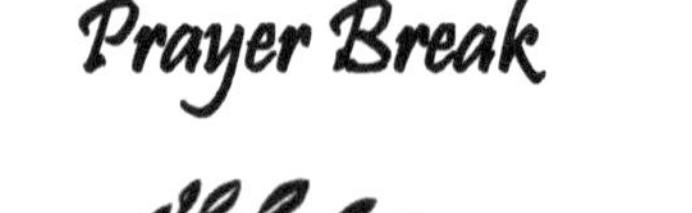

Prayer Break

Lord, You designed intimacy to be safe, mutual, and life-giving.
Teach us to love one another with self-sacrifice and respect,
and to speak words that heal rather than harm.
Remind us that our words carry power—
to build, to restore, or to wound.

Help us choose grace-filled, honest, and gentle communication,
even when conversations feel difficult.
Draw us into deeper intimacy—
not only in body, but in trust, understanding, and emotional
closeness. Let our connection be purposeful, pleasurable, and
protected, a bond that reflects Your design for marriage.

Amen.

Communication – Intimacy

Greg

Two qualities can elevate you in any situation: being teachable and learning to forgive not only others but yourself. It is sure that if you cannot learn from your mistakes, you will repeat them. When that occurs, you'll have a hard time forgiving yourself for your faults, which can lead to bitterness, anger, and feelings of loneliness or isolation (discussed later in this chapter). I am skilled at recognizing how I have sabotaged my relationships, and that understanding has helped me rebuild them.

Carolyn and I have been transparent throughout this book, and at times, you can see that I have been less than honest and that I faced character issues earlier in my life. Why am I resharing this now? In this chapter, we're discussing topics that might make you uncomfortable since it's not about major problems like infidelity, addictions, or even money issues. Yet, it's the small, unseen termites that can destroy a house without you even knowing it's happening. Small details become huge problems that eventually damage marriages. This is not just about divorce rates, because many people who have intimacy issues are still miserably married.

You may feel that as marriages grow and years pass, it is natural for certain things to fall away. You might have even felt superior when reading previous chapters, because you haven't had any of the issues we've discussed. You haven't cheated outside your marriage, you are financially stable as a household, and you have never manipulated or lied to your spouse. You may have even looked at your spouse and stated, "This book isn't for us. We don't have these problems. We're better than this."

It reminds me of a comical yet real-life incident involving a bishop as he sat on a plane en route to a conference. He looked around as he took his seat. The man across from him was already having an alcoholic drink, and they hadn't even taken off. Sighing in relief, the bishop thought, *Thank you, God, that's no longer me.*

He then stood and took off his jacket, noticing a man lighting up a cigarette (this was before you couldn't smoke on airplanes). The bishop thought, *Thank you, God, that is no longer me.*

He was feeling pretty good about being as righteous as he believed himself to be. He had overcome so much; these people around him needed Jesus.

As the plane ascended into the sky, the seat belt signs went off, and he slowly reclined his chair. He thought about calling his wife as soon as they landed.

But as he reclined, a beautiful young woman in the seat across and two aisles up was also reclining her seat. As her seat slowly went back, her dress inched higher and higher. Blinking, he watched her dress rise gradually, and sweat broke out on his forehead as he began to pray profusely and loudly. "Help me, Jesus, for I have sinned."

We can laugh together, but what the bishop needed us to understand, as he stood in the pulpit, was that just because I have not yet addressed your issue does not mean you are without problems. *Let he who is without sin cast the first stone.* John 8:7

Maybe the other chapters didn't hit you where you struggle, but this book is designed to find you where you truly are. And as you sit on the dock wondering how your boat drifted so far out to sea, Carolyn and I want to toss you a life raft.

Intimacy. Point-blank period.

Let's examine it, discuss what's killing it, and then restore it. We don't suddenly stop caring for and taking care of our spouse; we gradually drift away, like a boat in high tide that we failed to tie to the dock. We look up and see that the boat has floated too far to reach, leaving us alone on the pier, wondering why we didn't realize it was gone.

Ah, getting tossed a life raft makes sense now.

Carolyn

Greg is speaking from experience in our marriage. We lead by example, even in areas where you shouldn't follow. Let me share a typical night from a few years ago, when Greg had a side business in sales and was doing well. I watched him give his clients his full attention—staying on the phone, meeting them in person, texting into the night. I saw how he learned to read between the lines and identify needs they didn't even realize they had. However, I had a problem: he was not meeting *my* needs.

"Greg," I said as I prepared for bed, and he tapped away on his phone. I had tried to wait until he paused in his texting or emailing, but there was no pause I could jump into.

"Hmmm," he answered, without looking up.

"Greg," I said again. I was waiting for him to look up from his tapping so that I could talk to him.

"Yeah," he said, clearly not wanting to put his phone down.

"Greg!"

Finally, he looked at me as though I had lost my mind. "Carolyn, why are you snapping? What is it?"

Now, I'm upset, and I no longer want to talk to him—about anything. So, I flounced over, turning my back to him and angrily prepared to go to sleep.

I heard a huff behind my back, but Greg remained silent. I just knew he had gone back to his phone.

Carolyn had her back to me, and I was frustrated that she took me out of my workflow. I was getting things done. I was making money. My thoughts were that she should be glad I'm right here next to her, working. But as I lifted the phone to continue, I hesitated. I was starting to see myself, and I felt bad about it. I realized she had been trying to tell me something, and I wasn't listening.

Contrite, I leaned over and rubbed her back softly. "Babe, I apologize. What were you trying to tell me?"

Carolyn's back stiffened, but she answered softly. "Never mind, I accept your apology."

Her voice not only sounded soft but also alluring. And although we had not communicated earlier, I felt we could communicate differently now.

So, I scooted over and, rubbing her arm, soothed into her ear, "Turn over, babe."

"Not happening. Good night," she said.

BAM! Closed door.

Greg

If I close my eyes, I can still hear that emotional door slamming shut. What I had failed to realize was that intimacy doesn't begin at a physical touch like sex; it starts in the mind and emotions. As men, we tend to think nothing of ignoring our wives while the basketball or football game is on (although a lot of women are watching these days), or we just got home from work, and she wants to download her bad day, and we want to zone out.

There are so many demands on our time in today's social media-driven society that we don't connect in the home, and the connections we make on social media platforms like Facebook, TikTok, Instagram, Threads, YouTube, LinkedIn, Bluesky, X, or television aren't genuine. Device distractions are real, and they are damaging your intimacy with your spouse in several ways. Scrolling through your feeds is like trolling your spouse and family. Disconnect before you no longer have real people to turn to. Let's face it, you really don't have over two thousand friends.

Many Christian couples are living in intimacy deserts without understanding why. What if the path back to deep connection is more accessible than you've been led to believe?

Three common intimacy killers destroy connection: chronic distraction, unresolved conflicts that create emotional barriers, and unhealthy comparison to unrealistic standards. Part One of this chapter will deal with chronic distractions and unhealthy comparisons that set unrealistic standards.

I had an issue with shutting down my social media at the appropriate times. It wasn't that social media is evil, although evil does lurk there, but as a responsible adult, I had to learn how to use it without letting it use me. Carolyn and I have a podcast together, a website, and social media accounts, but we also have a greater intimacy. How did we do it? In correcting my missteps, I need to take out the devices I brought into it. In correcting my missteps, I need to minimize the distractions I brought into our bedroom. We need to figure out how to ensure the devices that can be advantageous when used correctly do not hinder us as a couple. How far down the rabbit hole were we? We needed to do an *Intimacy Barrier Audit*.

Intimacy Barrier Audit

Why It Matters:

Open communication between couples is established through intimacy. The level of trust determines the depth of intimacy, and trust grows strongest in places of safety—where ideas, goals, thoughts, and experiences can be shared without criticism or judgment. When distractions creep in—primarily through devices in the bedroom—they erode intimacy. To see how deeply these habits have taken root, you need to run an "audit." Dieters log their food to reveal mindless eating. In the same way, logging your habits shows where intimacy is being starved.

How to Apply It:

Conducting an "Intimacy Barrier Audit":

This exercise is to be completed by each of you separately. Don't cheat. Do as you always do. Just make a note of how long you are doing it.

- Track screen time in the bedroom for one week (devices create both physical and psychological barriers). The bedroom should be a place of rest, restoration, and connection. But when devices follow us into that sacred space, they divide our attention and build walls we don't even notice are being erected. By logging your screen time for a week, you'll get a clear picture of just how much space those glowing rectangles have stolen. Sometimes, seeing the numbers in black and white is what finally makes it real. It's not just about hours lost—it's about opportunities missed for conversation, laughter, quiet closeness, and physical touch.

- Identify unresolved conflicts that remain "off-limits" for discussion.(See section on Conflicts) Every marriage has subjects that feel like minefields—money, in-laws, intimacy, parenting styles. We avoid them, thinking silence equals peace, but silence only breeds distance. By writing these topics down during the audit, you bring them into the light. You're not expected to solve them right away—that's what the conflict resolution section will guide you through. But admitting they exist is the first step to disarming them. Think of it like marking the potholes on a road map: you can't fix what you won't name.

- Recognize comparison triggers (media, other couples, past relationships) that create unrealistic expectations. Comparison doesn't shout; it whispers. It sneaks in when you scroll through curated photos, when you hear how another couple spends their weekends, or when you secretly measure your spouse against someone from your past. Naming these triggers helps you see the trap before you fall into it. This step is about guarding your heart and your marriage from illusions that make you discontent with what's real. Once you recognize the lies comparison tells, you can choose truth: your spouse is who God chose for you, and your story together is worth honoring. The adage that "Comparison is the thief of joy" is accurate. The couple that you admire and follow on Instagram is the same couple that, when the lights go off, live separate lives. Stop scrolling and start paying attention to your spouse. No one should compare, and after you do the work in this book, they won't.

- Discuss findings with your spouse with an emphasis on *understanding*, not blame.

The audit isn't a weapon. It's not a scorecard to prove who's right or wrong. It's a mirror the two of you are holding up together to say, *"Here's where we are, and here's where we want to grow."* When you share what you've learned, lead with humility. Use inclusive language, starting sentences with *"I"* rather than a *"you"*-centric approach. This exercise is to heal the breach, not widen it. *"This is what I noticed about myself . . .*" rather than pointing fingers. Blame closes doors, but understanding opens them. When both spouses feel safe to admit struggles without fear of attack, trust deepens, intimacy flourishes, and you build a stronger foundation.

The Connection Ladder

Once you've identified and removed the barriers through your Intimacy Barrier Audit, the next step is to replace those wasted moments with habits that restore connection. Intimacy doesn't come back all at once—it grows in layers, like bricks building a wall of trust. That's why we call this practice the "Connection Ladder." Each rung takes you one step closer to the closeness you desire, but it's a climb you take together.

The Connection Ladder is a simple ten-minute evening ritual designed to rebuild intimacy through intentional, nonsexual touch, honest conversation, and spiritual unity. It's not about rushing back into physical intimacy, but about laying the foundation for trust, affection, and safety—step by step.

Why It Matters:

1 Corinthians 7:3–5 reminds us that husbands and wives owe each other physical intimacy, not as a demand but as a sacred duty of love. Yet, intimacy is more than sex—it is the daily choice to connect, body and soul. Couples can go years without a genuine connection, even if they live under the same roof. The Connection Ladder gives you a way back. By setting aside just ten minutes a night, you declare to your spouse: *"You matter more than my phone, my work, or my fatigue. You are my priority."*

How to Apply It:
The Ten-Minute Connection Ladder Evening Ritual

Minutes One–Three:
Share the highs and lows of your day while holding hands.

This is your starting rung. Sit face-to-face, hold hands, and share one highlight and one hardship from your day. The handholding grounds you—it's a physical reminder that you're not adversaries but allies. Keep it brief, but keep it honest. Vulnerability starts small, and sometimes all your spouse needs to hear is: *"This was hard for me today, but I'm glad I can tell you."*

Minutes Four–Six:
Exchange a three-minute shoulder massage while expressing appreciation.

This is the next rung up the ladder. Physical touch eases tension and lowers defenses. As you give your spouse a brief shoulder massage, say one thing you appreciate about them. It doesn't have to be grand— *"Thank you for making dinner tonight"* or *"I appreciate how hard you work for our family."* Appreciation spoken while giving a gentle touch reconditions the heart to feel safe in closeness again.

Minutes Seven–Nine:
Hold each other in a full embrace and breathe together.

This step slows you down. Wrap your arms around each other and take five deep breaths in unison. Feel your spouse's heartbeat, notice the rhythm of their breathing, and let your bodies sync. This is not a rushed hug before work or a distracted squeeze in passing. It's a deliberate pause. It says, *"In this moment, I am present with you."*

Minute Ten:
Pray together.

The final rung connects you both to God. Pray aloud, even if it feels awkward at first. Ask God to bless your marriage, heal old wounds, and protect your bond. Prayer is the glue that binds the other steps together—it turns vulnerability into strength, appreciation into gratitude, and touch into covenant love. When you invite God into those ten minutes, you're building intimacy on a foundation that cannot be shaken.

The Promise of the Connection Ladder

At first, it might feel mechanical or even uncomfortable. But over time, these ten minutes will become the most essential part of your day. As you climb the ladder nightly, you'll notice walls crumbling, laughter returning, and tenderness reigniting as you, once again, experience holding each other into the night. Intimacy doesn't have to be complicated—it only has to be intentional.

Note to Consider:

If this exercise doesn't work for you, and no matter what one person does, the other person dissolves into finger-pointing and microaggressions, consider individual counseling. Sometimes, it's really not you; it's them. And that is a difficult thing to realize: you can't fix it together because they have individual work to do.

You cannot go back and heal their childhood, no matter how many times they tell you, "You make me crazy." Or "Stop talking down to me." Or "If you did this better . . ." You should listen to your spouse's concerns as you dialogue in your connection time, and you should cross-correct on everything that you have heard them state during the ten-minute Ladder Connection that is correctable.

Example: If they no longer find you attractive, and you look the same with the exception that you've grown older, you can't turn back the clock. And perhaps their genuine concern is that *they* are growing older.

If your spouse (or you) is consistently unhappy, angry, or depressed, that also indicates a need for professional help. Sometimes, you won't require marital counseling; instead, individual therapy and support might be necessary.

Do the work with an open heart, but if you haven't moved closer to intimacy—not even an inch—after at least three months of starting this exercise, more intervention is needed.

This exercise and book are not a magical fix for the trauma that you or someone else may carry; that is the role of a trained trauma-informed care professional. *Trauma-informed care, trauma-informed practice, or trauma- and violence-informed care, is a framework for understanding and supporting people who have experienced adverse outcomes after exposure to harmful events.*

***

Communication When Silence is *not* Golden

Conflict Resolution

I cannot hold the belief that, as a man, I am the head of my household, yet fail to take responsibility for leading.

First of all, men, we have to understand that we are the drivers in a relationship. And for those women who are reading this too, when things are wrong, allow us room to autocorrect. Notice I didn't say "fix" it. We can't fix our problems; we can only correct our missteps. Notice I didn't say "mistakes." What may be unacceptable to Carolyn might be preferable to someone else's spouse. Learning my spouse, understanding her wants, meeting her needs is a job I took on when I said, "I do." Yes, I said *job*. Marriage is work. However, as with any other job, if you do it well, the benefits are endless, and retirement is Heaven on Earth.

When I correct my missteps, Carolyn sees me putting in effort. My willingness to be vulnerable builds her trust to be vulnerable too. We don't ever want to use those same vulnerabilities to hurt each other later. If Carolyn shares vulnerability with me, it's not a sledgehammer to be used against her at another time to make a point.

Example: Carolyn shared with me that she doesn't like massages. I didn't use this information during an argument about her having a real headache and not wanting to share intimacy. In my frustration of having my needs fulfilled, I didn't accuse her of being frigid or use her dislike of massages as proof of my claim. Doing so would breach her trust and be false, since Carolyn and I share incredible intimacy.

When couples use vulnerability as a hammer, especially at the beginning of a relationship, it is harder to establish trust. Without trust, it becomes impossible for the relationship to thrive in intimacy. And when trust is an issue, conflict becomes inevitable. It's that adage, "That's not what I said, but it is what you heard."

Do You Hear What I Said—Seeds of Conflict

Carolyn's relationship with her siblings was always close and loving. They might disagree, but they remained connected. My upbringing was different. Having to act as the secondary parent in a single-parent household made me take on the role of disciplinarian instead of big brother. I was assigned the role of the man of the house at a very young age and was responsible for my younger siblings. When a position that you are not ready to fill occurs, conflict is inevitable. I didn't have the wisdom, experience, or patience to parent. As a result, resentment from my siblings set in, and to this day, we are still finding our path.

Why mention this? Because Carolyn and I filter our knowledge through different lenses based on our childhood experiences. Even with good intentions, our differences collide.

Let me set the scene:

Carolyn walked into the room, looking tired, purse in hand. "Greg, I have to go pick up my sister and then go to Mom's."

I replied, sharper than I intended, "Okay, but you've been going over there every day for the last two weeks, and the situation hasn't changed. I know you want to help, but how about skipping a day so we can watch a movie or go out to lunch?"

She sighed, shaking her head. "It doesn't matter how many days I've gone. If they need me, I'm going. We can go out for dinner if you'd like."

I bristled. "No, Carolyn. I have some phone appointments this evening. You do what you've already set your mind to do."

Placing her purse on the counter, she squinted at me, frowning. "You don't understand. Maybe you're not close to your siblings . . ."

And just like that, within five minutes, we were immersed in conflict.

What happened? I was worried she was overdoing it, but what she heard was criticism of her relationship with her siblings. And because of my background—always feeling "last" in my household, her prioritizing her family felt like abandonment—one exchange, two interpretations, and suddenly . . . distance.

Why It Matters:

Conflict is inevitable in marriage, but how we communicate during it determines whether it divides or unites us. Research shows that 69 percent of marital conflicts are never fully resolved (*The Seven Principles for Making Marriage Work*, Dr. John Gottman, Gottman Institute).[24] Yet couples who learn healthy resolution skills thrive because they manage tension rather than letting it control them.

Proverbs 15:1 reminds us: "*A gentle answer turns away wrath, but a harsh word stirs up anger.*"

Carolyn

Our words can be weapons, or they can be bridges. Conflict resolution is not about avoiding arguments; many breakthroughs in relationships result from healthy conflict. Then why are so many people afraid of disputes? It's because we have been taught, especially as women, that conflict is destructive. So, we try to avoid it. We push thoughts down, beliefs away, and stay silent in the face of others' preferences. As a result, we are a society full of stress, unhappiness, depression, and unhealthy addictions. These addictions are often our attempt to self-medicate, a placebo that only masks, not resolves, our issues. Healthy conflict resolved positively in marriage is about transforming differences into opportunities for intimacy, understanding, and growth.

Why It Matters:

Destructive Impact

- Assumptions obscure clarity. Each spouse hears what they fear, not what was actually said. How many times have you been baffled when your spouse states you said something that you never said? It's not that they're a liar; it's what landed through their filter and was heard.

---

[24] Gottman, John. Seven Principles for Making Marriage Work. Gottman Institute

- Withdrawal follows escalation. Instead of resolving the issue, one or both partners pull back emotionally or physically.

- As stated earlier, we often pull back from asserting ourselves respectfully and succinctly because we have been taught that conflict is wrong. Or we have seen our parents in destructive patterns that we intend to break by staying silent and not engaging. It is like feeling you have cleaned your house by closing the door to the clutter and dirt.

Old wounds resurface. Childhood experiences and past hurts get tangled in present disagreements, intensifying the conflict. We are all a product of our past—a compilation of our environments and experiences. When we decide that our childhood household did it is the only way to do it, we set ourselves up for unhealthy conflict.

It reminds me of the story of a young daughter-in-law who wanted to please her husband by cooking just as his mother did. She stood by her mother-in-law's side, overseeing her process as she prepared the family ham. To her surprise, the older woman sliced off both ends of the ham and then placed the remainder in the oven, leaving two good pieces of meat discarded on a plate.

Trying not to offend, the young wife asked gently, "Mother, why do you cut off both ends of the ham?"

With a confident tilt of her head, the mother-in-law replied, "My dear, this is how it's done."

Still puzzled, the daughter-in-law pressed, "But where did the recipe come from?"

"Why, from my mother, of course," came the firm response.

Determined to prove the tradition, the mother-in-law called her own mother on speakerphone. "Hello, Mother. Can you explain to our newlywed why we cut off both ends of the ham before cooking it?"

A soft chuckle drifted through the line. "Well, baby, back in those days, it was simply because our oven was too small."

Unchecked, these patterns create cycles that damage trust and erode intimacy.

Healing Action Steps: Building a Conflict Resolution Map for Marriage

1. Pause & Pray

Before diving into the issue, take two minutes to pray together. *Don't pray to change them; pray for resolution.* Philippians 4:6–7 (NLT): "Don't worry about anything; instead, pray about everything . . . Then you will experience God's peace."

2. Listen to Understand, Not to React

One spouse shares while the other only listens—no interruptions. Then switch. Repeat back what you heard: "What I hear you saying is . . ." James 1:19 (NLT): "Be quick to listen, slow to speak, and slow to get angry."

3. Ask:

"Is this about today, or is there something deeper?" Don't fight about dishes or bills—those are surface issues. The real question is often hidden beneath the surface.

We can keep rehashing what happened ten years ago, or we can examine why the circumstances from then are resurfacing now and how they impact our marriage today.

For example: *"You had an affair ten years ago, and yes, I forgave you. But when you start coming home late without explanation, it feels like a repeat of that painful season. Can you please let me know where you are, and if I call, can you answer? That reassurance helps me trust that the past isn't repeating itself."*

By naming the more profound fear, you move beyond symptoms and speak to the heart of the issue.

Proverbs 20:5 (NLT) reminds us: "Though good advice lies deep within the heart, a person with understanding will draw it out."

4. Choose "Us" Over "Me"

Remember: it's not you vs. me; it's us vs. the problem. *There's nothing like knowing you are on the same team and that even your pain is shared.* Ephesians 5:21 (NLT): "Submit to one another out of reverence for Christ."

5. Brainstorm Practical Solutions

Each person offers one idea to move forward. Agree on the next steps—budgeting, date nights, chore division, and counseling. *I once heard it said that two heads are not better than one; it's a two-headed monster. You both can't lead at the same time. It is the man's responsibility to know when his best foot forward is not as good as hers. Agree to discuss the issue and choose the next course of action, hers or his. Here, you may ask, 'What if we still don't agree?" Then go back to step one and pray about it.*
Amos 3:3 (NLT): "Can two people walk together without agreeing on the direction?"

6. Forgive & Let Go

Say the words: "I forgive you. I release this from my heart." Don't resurrect old conflicts once forgiveness is given.

Colossians 3:13 (NLT): "Make allowance for each other's faults and forgive anyone who offends you."

7. Seal It with Prayer & Affection

After coming up with a solution, pray again, asking God to bless your agreement. End with a hug, kiss, or physical touch. *Let the joy of what's inside come outside into a building of intimacy through physical touch.* Ecclesiastes 4:12 (NLT): "A triple-braided cord is not easily broken."

Real-Life Example:
The Power of a Pause

During one of our most stressful financial seasons, Carolyn and I found ourselves in another heated discussion. My instinct was to react defensively: "You're always on me about money!" Instead, I stopped, prayed silently, and said, "I feel overwhelmed, and I don't want to fight you. Can we look at this together?"

The argument was defused instantly. Same stress, different response. That pause created space for connection instead of destruction.

Closing Reflection:

Conflict resolution is not about avoiding fights; it's about fighting the right way, together. When we paused to pray, listened with empathy, and reminded ourselves that we were on the same team, our conflicts became open doors instead of stone walls.

Every couple will argue. But not every couple will grow from it. The difference lies in choosing to respond with grace rather than react with anger. The steps outlined above are the very ones your worksheets will guide you through—turning biblical principles into daily practice.

Listen to Podcast #35 On Apple or Spotify: Why Your Marriage Isn't Growing/Why You Feel Like Roommates in Your Christian Marriage and How to Rebuild Real Intimacy
Link: https://why-your-marriage-isnt-growing.captivate.fm/

Chapter 8:
Intimacy - Worksheet

Emotional Safety, Spiritual Unity, and Trust

Key Principle

True intimacy is more than physical closeness, emotional safety, spiritual unity, and trust built through vulnerability.

Reflection Questions:

1. What small daily habit makes me feel most connected to you?

Write it here:

____

____

____

2. When do I feel safest to share my heart with you?

Write it here:

____

____

____

The Connection Ladder—Practice Steps

Creating Safe Spaces for Connection

Set aside daily time to connect without distractions. Devices off, hearts on. (Song of Solomon 2:14)

What's one fifteen-minute window we can protect each day for connection?

____

Practice Intentional Touch

Use nonsexual touch—holding hands, hugging, resting your head on their shoulder—to affirm love. (Mark 10:8)

List two ways you can show love through touch this week:

Share Vulnerabilities, Not Weapons

When your spouse opens up, respond with compassion, not critique. (1 Peter 4:8)

Write one area you will share more openly about:

To download or use the fillable online worksheet, please go to our Married With A Purpose website: ttvttg.com

Multiple Choice Check-In– Check the correct answer

1. What is intimacy according to this chapter?

a) Just physical closeness

b) Emotional safety, spiritual unity, and trust

c) Avoiding conflict

d) Spending money together

2. Which scripture encourages us to show deep love because "love covers a multitude of sins"?

a) Proverbs 24:26

b) 1 Peter 4:8

c) Matthew 18:20

d) Mark 10:8

3. Which daily practice can build intimacy the most effectively?

a) Setting aside time without distractions

b) Arguing less

c) Planning vacations

d) Avoiding deep topics

Closing Reflection:

What is one small way you can nurture intimacy this week? Write down an action you can take to strengthen emotional and spiritual closeness.

____

____

Chapter 8:
Conflict Resolution – Worksheet

Communication: From Reacting to Responding

Key Principle

It's not you vs. me. It's us vs. the problem.

Reflection Questions:

1. When was the last time a five-minute conversation escalated into conflict for us?

____

____

____

2. Which of our childhood "filters" (past experiences, family patterns) most often shape how we hear each other?

____

____

____

Conflict Resolution Map—Practice Steps

Pause & Pray

Take two minutes to ask God for peace, patience, and perspective.

How could pausing for prayer have changed our last conflict?

____

____

____

Listen to Understand

Repeat back what you heard: "What I hear you saying is . . ."

Practice here:

Spouse 1 says: _______________________________________

Spouse 2 repeats: _____________________________________

Define the *Real* Issue

Our last fight was about

____,

but the deeper issue was

____

Multiple Choice Check-In—Check the correct answer

1. What is the FIRST step in the Conflict Resolution Map?

    a) Define the Real Issue

    b) Pause & Pray

    c) Forgive & Let Go

    d) Choose "Us" Over "Me."

2. Which scripture reminds us to be "quick to listen, slow to speak, and slow to get angry"?

    a) James 1:19

    b) Proverbs 20:5

    c) Colossians 3:13

    d) Ephesians 5:21

3. After reaching a resolution, what is the final step?

a) Seal it with Prayer & Affection

b) Forgive & Let Go

c) Brainstorm Solutions

d) Pause & Pray

Closing Reflection:

What step from the Conflict Resolution Map do we most need to practice this week?

____

____

____

____

____

____

To download or use the fillable online worksheet, please go to our Married With A Purpose website: ttvttg.com

Chapter 9

Blended Families—Becoming One Without Breaking Apart

Gregory

As a stepparent to Carolyn's sons, I felt the responsibility of stepping into a family dynamic that already had its rhythm. I also had the added obstacle of having once been married to Carolyn and failing her. Everyone knows that when you hurt a boy's mother, you will face their wrath. Because Carolyn and I want to be respectful of others in our narratives, I won't share an anecdote about the problems I encountered while reblending. But I will tell you that I had an uphill battle to carry. There were many conversations filled with anger and resentment that we had to get through. Regaining trust after losing it is more complex than anything. Remember, I was doing this while showing Carolyn that remarriage was a good thing. She already trusted me, but her sons didn't have that same confidence. Before me was a mountain, and I was carrying it with past baggage on my back.

If this is you, and you're climbing that mountain, keep going, keep praying, and believing that God can heal the breach. I never wanted to disrupt what was already sacred between a mother and her children, but I also knew I was called to be more than just a bystander. But this time, as a true believer, I had God on my side and His word as my weapon. I understood that, regardless of what it looked like, this was not Mission Impossible, and that my goal to provide guidance and stability, and a model of godly leadership, was attainable.

When conflicts arose, Carolyn and I decided early on to address them as a team. Sometimes, she took the lead; other times, I did, but always with the intention of presenting a united front. Over time, my relationship with the boys shifted from that of an outside interloper to something much more profound. I wasn't just "Mom's husband." I became a father figure, dependable, and intentional. I wanted them to see a man who would stand firm in integrity, no matter what life stage they were in. I also wanted them to see that if you are on the wrong path, you can correct your trajectory and change your course for the better.

Carolyn

My journey was about reconciliation and respect. You've read our beginning chapters, and you know what a challenge it was for me to accept Gregory's infidelity. I wasn't going to be able to sweep it under the table; a child was conceived. Remarrying and understanding that not only was Greg going to have to reintroduce himself into my family unit, but I was also going to have to do the same.

It took longer than I would have liked, but when I came into Greg's son's life, he was around four or five years old. I understood that his mother's role was already firmly established, and my task was not to replace her but to build my own bond with him carefully. That didn't happen overnight. It took over a year of patience, prayer, and intentional love before trust began to take root. It was not easy, but children at that age are more able to trust than older children if the adults involved allow them.

Years later, as an adult, He and his bride asked me, as an elder in the church, to perform their wedding. At first, I hesitated, knowing the weight of what that meant. As a mother myself, I know how deeply significant that role is. After much prayer, I agreed—choosing love above hesitation. My bonus-son made his stance clear: his mother would not be attending, and nothing would be allowed to disturb the joy of the day.

Greg and I walked with them through the planning, the venue visit, the food tasting, and the anticipation leading up to the celebration. On the wedding day, the weather was perfect, the setting breathtaking, and the joy undeniable. One of the most moving moments for me was dancing with him during the mother-son dance. It was a moment of joy, redemption, and deep connection.

Now, as "Grandmom" to our grandson, his son—the youngest boy of our seven grandchildren—I see how that early bond has expanded into a legacy of love.

Caroyln and Gregory

Blending our families was never simple. It meant striking a balance between respect and responsibility, humility and leadership, and prayer and action. We had to learn patience, to yield when necessary, and to step forward when called.

Looking back, we see how God worked through the challenges, weaving our separate lives into a single legacy. Today, we are not only parents and grandparents, but also partners who continue to model love, faith, and consistency for our family.

What began as two distinct journeys has become one story—rooted in grace, strengthened through trials, and flourishing across generations. In this chapter, we will guide you through the steps we took and continue to take to make our family not just work, but thrive.

Why It Matters:

You've fallen in love . . . again. It didn't work last time, and this time, you have considerations you didn't have before: children. You have more to lose because more people are involved. You can't mess this up; your heart couldn't take it, and neither could your children's.

Carolyn and I understand that blending families is one of the most significant challenges couples can face. It's not just about love between two people. It's about building trust across entire households, navigating stepparenting dynamics, and respecting loyalties that already exist. Without intentionality, children can feel torn, spouses can feel unappreciated, and what should be a fresh start can become a battlefield. That's why it matters because a marriage covenant isn't only about two lives. It can set the tone for generations.

How to Apply It:

Unified Parenting Approach:

Decide discipline strategies in private before applying them. The only way this works is if you plan, follow through, and heal from any past baggage through premarital counseling. The two of you getting on the same page will be necessary to align your two families. Learning from past mistakes and deciding how to move forward together is crucial. A unified, well-thought-out household plan not only provides you both with boundaries and guidelines, but it also fosters a sense of safety for the entire household. Children like knowing what to expect and when to expect it.

But suppose you acquired this book after you got married, and everything is falling apart because none of the preparatory work was done? Then, finding a family counselor that you both can agree on is crucial. This will take courage. It's challenging and uncomfortable to hear how you've done things wrong. But confronting your shortcomings and others sharing theirs is the beginning of healing. Many years ago, I read Randy Shankle's book *Merismos*, in which he discussed change. I've never forgotten it. It described the process of change in three stages:

Stage One: *Revelation*, where you realize that change is needed;

Stage Two: *Transformation*, where you begin the process of changing what you have revealed; and

Stage Three: *Manifestation*, when you, as a family, are walking in the transformation of all of your work.

So, to have a healthy family, just like a healthy marriage, you must choose to change.

Family Meetings:

Hold regular times where every member has a voice. Once you're done, and you're walking in a unified front as a family, checking in is necessary. Holding family meetings is not just about sharing the negative; it is also about celebrating the positive. When everyone knows that they have a place to be heard, people are empowered and move through the world with God-given confidence.

Defined Roles:

Early on, let the biological parent take the lead in discipline, with the stepparent standing in support. You'll find that discipline without relationship almost always breeds rebellion. A friend once told Carolyn and me that her mother, Dorothy, gave her this advice when she got engaged to a man who had a daughter: *"If you can't hug her, you can't discipline her."* That stayed with me. It was a reminder that love has to lead the way.

Blending a family takes time—you can't rush it. That includes stepping into the role of parent before a proper place has been made for you. But here's the good news: if you've laid the groundwork, if you've done the hard work in the steps above, then what you're facing isn't impossibility. It's simply a matter of time.

Grace & Patience:

Relationships take time—don't push; let love develop organically. This step is easy to state, but harder to do. This is the step where faith and prayer work together intermittently. You must believe that, in most cases, the process will work. If it doesn't, then you may find yourself in a situation where you have to make some difficult decisions about your new marriage. Above all, have hope; the two of you can scale mountains together.

New Traditions:

Blend old customs into new ones that reflect your family's unique identity. One of the most fun things a family can do is create their own traditions. Planning new ways to celebrate your holidays and milestones can be freeing for everyone involved. An annual trip to the apple orchard, returning home, and making cider and pies is a great way to celebrate back-to-school for the kids.

Celebrate Small Wins:

A smile, a kind word, or a peaceful dinner are signs of progress worth noting.

Exes and in-Laws

Blending families doesn't happen in a vacuum. Even if you and your spouse are doing the hard work to knit your home together, there are often outside forces pressing in. Sometimes, those forces are the very people who should be cheering you on.

Problematic in-laws can be one of the trickiest trials. Maybe they never thought you were the "right one" for their son or daughter. Perhaps they resent the influence you now have in the children's lives. Instead of supporting your marriage, they quietly—or not so quietly—undermine it. Their subtle comments, lack of respect, or outright hostility can plant seeds of division in a blended home if you're not careful. What's needed here is firm boundaries. Respect is due to parents, yes, but not at the expense of your marriage. You and your spouse must protect the covenant you've built, presenting the same united front with extended family that you do with the children inside your home.

"That is why a man leaves his father and mother and is united to his wife, and they become one flesh."—Genesis 2:24 (NIV)

And then there are exes. Not every coparent wants to see your new marriage thrive. Some will stir conflict, feeding children's insecurity, or try to keep one foot in a household that no longer belongs to them. Others act out of hurt, using manipulation or anger to disrupt the peace you've fought for. In these moments, patience and prayer are not optional—they are survival. You may not be able to change their behavior, but you can control your response. Always put the children first, keep communication respectful and clear, and refuse to let bitterness take root.

- *"If it is possible, as far as it depends on you, live at peace with everyone."*— Romans 12:18 (NIV)

A reminder that peace may not always be reciprocated, but your responsibility is to maintain it as far as it depends on you.

- *"Do not be overcome by evil, but overcome evil with good."*—Romans 12:21 (NIV)→This speaks to not letting bitterness or manipulation take root in your home.

Closing Reflection:

Blending families is not simply about two adults choosing love. It is about shaping a home where children, histories, traditions, and expectations learn how to live together. Without intention, this merging can create strain and resentment. With patience and grace, it can grow into stability, unity, and genuine affection.

Remember: in every endeavor, your word is your weapon.

Using the word as a weapon means bringing truth to the table, not just facts. This distinction matters more than we often realize. Families can become trapped in debating facts while missing the truth beneath them. When a family member raises an issue, the aim is not to prepare a rebuttal but to listen for what is truly being said.

Consider this example. Johnny receives a new bike as a reward for outstanding grades. Steven, however, works just as hard but does not achieve the same academic results. The facts say Johnny earned his bike. That is accurate. The truth, though, may be that Steven will never compete with Johnny in the classroom, nor should he be expected to. His effort still carries weight.

The question then becomes this: where does Steven shine? What lane does he run well in? When families take the time to recognize different strengths, success is no longer measured by comparison. It is measured by growth, effort, and fairness. That truth creates dignity. And dignity builds trust, which every blended family needs to survive and thrive.

"From him the whole body, joined and held together by every supporting ligament, grows and builds itself up in love, as each part does its work."— Ephesians 4:16 (NIV)→ This reminds us that a family is not made strong by perfection, but by connection. Each member is valued, each role matters, and together they are held in love—not flawless, but faithfully and purposefully blended.

Chapter 9:
Blended Families Questions & Answers – Worksheet

Real-Life Questions & Answers

Q: How do we build trust with stepchildren?

Answer:

____

____

____

- **Practical Tip:** Don't force relationships—allow bonds to form naturally.

- **Scripture:** *"Love is patient and kind . . ."* (1 Corinthians 13:4 NLT)

Q: How do we handle discipline when the children aren't biologically yours?

Answer:

____

____

____

- **Practical Tip:** The biological parent leads discipline early, with the stepparent reinforcing.

- **Scripture:** *"If a house is divided against itself, that house cannot stand."* **(Mark 3:25 (NIV)**

Q: How do we deal with different traditions, rules, or expectations?

Answer:

____

____

____

- **Practical Tip:** Create fresh traditions together.

- ***Scripture:*** *"Make every effort to keep yourselves united in the Spirit, binding yourselves together with peace." (Ephesians 4:3 NLT)*

Q: What if one child resists the new marriage?

Answer:

____

____

____

- **Practical Tip:** Give them space to feel their emotions and listen without defensiveness.

- **Scripture:** *"He heals the brokenhearted and binds up their wounds."* **(Psalm 147:3 NIV)**

Q: How do we manage finances in a blended household?

Answer:

____

____

____

- **Practical Tip:** Draft a family budget that meets the needs of all children.

- **Scripture:** *"Suppose one of you wants to build a tower. Won't you first sit down and estimate the cost to see if you have enough money to complete it?"* **(Luke 14:28 NIV)**

Q: How do we keep our marriage first without children feeling left out?

Answer:

____

____

____

- **Practical Tip:** Schedule regular "couple time" and treat it as sacred, not optional. Let the kids see that love is nurtured through intention.

- **Scripture:** *"That is why a man leaves his father and mother and is joined to his wife, and the two are united into one." (Genesis 2:24 NLT)*

Chapter 9:
Blended Families - Worksheet

Reflection: Share Your Story

Write about your personal experience with blended families. What challenges and blessings have you seen?

____

____

____

Worksheet Questions – Check the correct answers

1. How can trust best be built with stepchildren?

a) By demanding immediate respect

b) By allowing love and trust to grow over time

c) By giving gifts as a substitute for presence

d) By limiting time with their biological parent

2. When it comes to discipline in blended families, the best approach is:

a) The stepparent takes complete control immediately

b) Children decide consequences themselves

c) Biological parents lead discipline; stepparent supports

d) Discipline should be avoided

3. How should different family traditions be handled?

a) Choose one family's traditions

b) Ignore old traditions

c) Blend traditions and create new ones together

d) Avoid traditions

4. If a child resists the new marriage, what should parents do?

a) Ignore the child's feelings

b) Reassure and listen patiently

c) Force acceptance

d) Blame the child

5. What is one way to manage finances in a blended family?

a) Keep finances private

b) Create a family budget for all children

c) Handle finances separately

d) Spend first, discuss later

List two or three new traditions you could create:

____

____

List one way you can celebrate small wins as a family:

____

____

Closing Reflection:

Blended families require patience, unity, and intentional grace. Reflect on how these principles can strengthen your home.

____

____

Prayer Break

Lord, as we come to the end of this book,
We do not go back to old, unfruitful ways or stop the work in
progress you have begun in this marriage. For He who has begun a
good work, shall see it finished.

Give us the courage to move from reading to doing:
to complete the worksheets,
to communicate honestly,
and to work toward deeper intimacy.

Guide us as we blend our families according to Your will,
establish healthy boundaries,
and speak to one another with respect and honor.

Teach us to work while there is yet day.
Guard us from delay and distraction,
and help us steward this moment with intention,
before the opportunity passes.

And, if further intervention is needed, give us the courage,
finances, and resources to seek one-on-one help.

We place our marriage, our family,
and our future in Your hands.

Amen.

Chapter 10

Twice the Vows, Twice the Grace

Marriage is not about perfection. It's about persistence. It's waking up each morning and choosing each other, even when the choosing feels heavy. It's about grace that covers failure, love that keeps no record of wrongs, forgiveness on repeat, and faith that looks beyond the brokenness to see what God is still building.

Our story proves that failure doesn't have to be final. We walked through betrayal, divorce, and despair. We faced addictions, lies, financial struggles, spiritual division, and the jagged edges of blending a family. And yet—here we stand. Not because we were strong enough, but because grace was greater.

"Twice the Vows. Twice the Grace." That's not just a title. It's our testimony.

When we said "I do" the first time, we didn't know what storms awaited us. We weren't equipped, we weren't anchored, and our baggage outweighed our preparation. But by the second time, God had given us eyes to see. The vows were no longer words spoken in the throes of romance and fairy tales. They were promises forged in fire and renewed through God's mercy.

And isn't that what grace does? It doesn't erase the past; it redeems it. It doesn't pretend the scars aren't there; it makes them holy reminders of where God stepped in. We began this journey by sharing our biggest failures, but our prayer is that you will take away from this book the understanding that nothing is too hard for God.

Twice The Vows Twice The Grace

If your marriage is on the brink, hear this: *you are not alone*. If your marriage is in repair, remember this: *healing takes time*. If your marriage is thriving, don't coast, keep building, keep praying, keep hoping, and keep loving. Wherever you are, know that there is always more grace available.

Remember: God, who resurrected us, can resurrect you. The dry bones of your marriage will live. Breathe on them with the heartfelt belief that there is life after chaos, trauma, and damage. And when your hearts start pumping in sync once more, your new song will soar.

Chapter 10:
Renewing the Covenant - Worksheet

Reflection: Where do you see God's grace in your marriage story?

Questions to Answer Together:

1. What are three lessons you've learned from the struggles we've faced in this marriage?

____

____

____

____

____

2. What boundaries or commitments do we need to set to protect our marriage moving forward?

____

____

____

____

____

3. How will we invite God into our daily marriage rhythm?

____

____

____

____

____

Action Step:

Writing Your Renewal Vows

Take a quiet moment together. Write new vows—simple, personal, and rooted in grace. Speak them aloud. Let them mark the fresh covenant you are choosing today.

____

____

____

____

____

Closing Reflection:

This is not the end of your story. It's the beginning of a stronger one. _Twice the Vows. Twice the Grace._ We believe that your marriage will be a living testimony of love that performs as God intended. We are supernaturally praying and fasting every week for every person and couple who pick up this book in faith, not only to read it but also to apply its principles.

We have a weekly podcast that can amplify our message, and we are certified marriage coaches who can help you beyond these written pages. We invite you to contact us through our website, where we can connect our faith with yours and build Kingdom marriages that can save our communities.

You came this far—don't stop at the last page. Click the link to download the printable worksheets and a few thoughtfully prepared resources. Subscribe to our website for access. No inbox noise—just support for your marriage, poured with care. ttvttg.com

Worksheet Answer Key

Chapter 5

1. B
2. C
3. C
4. A

Chapter 6

1. B
2. B
3. B
4. B
5. A

Chapter 7 – Self-Directed

Chapter 8

1. B
2. B
3. A

Chapter 8, Conflict Resolution

1. B
2. A
3. A

Chapter 9

Real-Life Questions & Answers

Q: How do we build trust with stepchildren?

- **Answer:** Trust is earned, not demanded. Create safe spaces for love to grow.

Q: How do we handle discipline when the children aren't biologically yours?

- **Answer:** Discipline should be united and consistent.

Q: How do we deal with different traditions, rules, or expectations?

- **Answer:** Blending means respecting the past, creating new family rhythms.

Q: What if one child resists the new marriage?

- **Answer:** Remind them they are not being replaced.

Q: How do we manage finances in a blended household?

- **Answer:** Money issues need transparency and early planning.

Q: How do we keep our marriage first without children feeling left out?

- **Answer:** A strong marriage builds the safe foundation children long for.
  Chapter Nine—Conflict Resolution

1. B
2. C
3. C
4. B
5. B

Chapter 10 - Self-Directed

About the Authors

Pastor Gregory L. Napier and Evangelist Carolyn Napier are the founders of *Married with a Purpose* and co-leaders of *Never Ending Word Ministry*, an online church dedicated to spreading the Gospel of Jesus Christ worldwide. Married for over thirty-six years—with a powerful testimony of divorce, reconciliation, and remarriage—they stand as living proof that God can take what was broken and make it stronger than ever.

Gregory, a former U.S. Marine and retired postal worker with twenty-five years of service, answered the call to ministry after a divine encounter that ended his season of running from God. Born in the projects of Tennessee, he carries a deep passion for discipleship, biblical teaching, and helping others walk boldly in their purpose.

Carolyn, a compassionate teacher and encourager, has dedicated her life to helping women and families navigate challenges with faith and grace. Her heart for ministry beats for transformation—turning pain into purpose and trials into testimonies. Together, the Napiers share a mission to restore marriages, revive families, and renew faith through books, marriage coaching, podcasts, and speaking engagements. Their ministry blends biblical wisdom, practical strategies, and authentic transparency—offering couples a road map to thrive, not just survive, in love.

They are the proud parents of a blended family, grandparents to seven beautiful grandchildren, and passionate advocates for strong family values rooted in Christ. Whether they're preaching from the pulpit, recording their podcast, or sitting at the kitchen table counseling a couple in crisis, their message remains unwavering: God's grace is enough to heal, restore, and strengthen any marriage.

Twice The Vows Twice The Grace

Pastor Gregory Napier and

Evangelist Carolyn Napier

Certified Marriage Coaches